THE SAVVY MIDLIFER'S GUIDE TO DECLUTTERING

CLEAR THE CLUTTER, RECLAIM YOUR SANITY, AND CREATE SPACE FOR THE LIFE YOU WANT!

CAT COLUCCIO

© **Copyright 2023 - All rights reserved.**

The content contained within this book may not be reproduced, duplicated or transmitted without direct written permission from the author or the publisher.

Under no circumstances will any blame or legal responsibility be held against the publisher, or author, for any damages, reparation, or monetary loss due to the information contained within this book, either directly or indirectly.

Legal Notice:

This book is copyright protected. It is only for personal use. You cannot amend, distribute, sell, use, quote or paraphrase any part, or the content within this book, without the consent of the author or publisher.

Disclaimer Notice:

Please note the information contained within this document is for educational and entertainment purposes only. All effort has been executed to present accurate, up to date, reliable, complete information. No warranties of any kind are declared or implied. Readers acknowledge that the author is not engaged in the rendering of legal, financial, medical or professional advice. The content within this book has been derived from various sources. Please consult a licensed professional before attempting any techniques outlined in this book.

By reading this document, the reader agrees that under no circumstances is the author responsible for any losses, direct or indirect, that are incurred as a result of the use of the information contained within this document, including, but not limited to, errors, omissions, or inaccuracies.

CONTENTS

Introduction	vii
1. CLUTTER—THE NEMESIS TO YOUR BEST LIFE!	1
Skeletons	1
The Effects of Clutter on Self-Perception and Self-Esteem	4
The Effects of Clutter on Work and Productivity	6
The Effects of Clutter on Health and Wellness	7
Challenging Minimalism	7
2. WHAT MATTERS TO YOU?	11
Visualization: Your Secret Sauce	12
Minimalist, Simplified, or Organized	13
Hoarders in Real Time	15
3. PHYSICAL CLUTTER—A WALK THROUGH YOUR BEDROOMS, BATHROOMS, ENTRY, AND LIVING AREAS	19
Celebrate Small Wins	19
Energy and Motivation	20
The Inner Sanctum	22
The Royal Flush	28
Entryways and Living Spaces	31
4. PHYSICAL CLUTTER—A WALK THROUGH YOUR KITCHEN, LAUNDRY ROOM, AND GARAGE	35
The Drop Zone	36
It's a Wash	40
No Parking Zone	42
A Few Toss, Keep, or Donate Rules and Suggestions	46
5. DIGITAL CLUTTER—A WALK THROUGH YOUR COMPUTERS, TABLETS, AND PHONES	49
Information Overload	49
We Interrupt This Program…	50
Tips to Manage Digital Clutter	53

6. MENTAL CLUTTER—SMASHING YOUR LIMITING BELIEFS, INNER CRITIC, AND NEGATIVE INNER CHATTER — 59
   Mental Chatter and Overwhelm — 60
   Survivor's Guilt — 62
   The Impact of Mental Clutter — 64
   Clarity and Kindness — 66

7. YOUR WORKPLACE—PHYSICAL, DIGITAL, AND MENTAL DECLUTTERING AND PRODUCTIVITY TIPS — 73
   Work-Related — 74
   Liberating Your Desk — 75
   Mementos and Miscellaneous — 77
   Sensory Distractions — 79

8. RELEASING THE PAST — 85
   Emotional Distraction — 85
   Memory Keepers and the Guilty Conscience — 86
   Swedish Death Cleaning — 88
   Letting Go — 92

9. MAINTENANCE SYSTEMS AND TIPS — 95
   Understanding Yourself — 95
   Drawing the Line — 97
   More Organization Tips — 99

10. CREATING THE LIFE YOU WANT — 105
    Where to Next—Your Personal Life Audit — 105
    Building Blocks—Auditing Your Attitude, Time, and Attention — 109
    Positivity and the Perfect Day — 113

    Conclusion — 115
    References — 119
    About Cat — 123

Dedicated to

*Those who are ready to lose their burden of "stuff"
-be it emotional, physical or digital-
so they can fully embrace their next season of life with freedom and joy.*

INTRODUCTION

While you may not qualify for an episode of *Hoarders*, if you are struggling with clutter anywhere in your home, on your devices, or in your head, then Houston, *we have a problem!*

When some people hear the word *minimalism*, they automatically think of living in a tent, cooking over an open fire, limiting technology, and avoiding social contact. In their minds, to be a minimalist means you have to get rid of all your worldly possessions and live off the land. They think if they scale down, they will end up living like the contestants on the reality television shows *Survivor* and *Naked and Afraid*. But what minimalism is really about is getting rid of the clutter in your life that keeps you from thinking clearly and moving with purpose. It's about reclaiming your sanity and creating space for the things you really want in life.

I admit it. I am a recovering clutter-holic. I was once a high school teacher and then a lecturer with a tendency to collect piles of resources. I launched multiple businesses, was a professional musician, and dabbled in various artistic pursuits. Experimentation is my personal passion, but, because I love learning, I am also prone to collecting clutter in the process. I enjoy learning and

INTRODUCTION

trying new things, but I have struggled with the stuff that accumulates with each new venture. I learned the hard way how clutter negatively affects productivity, creativity, and morale, especially in your midlife season when there is already so much going on.

My decluttering journey is a work in progress. Along the way, I've discovered tips to help you put your life in order, and I've conducted a great deal of research to understand more about the impact of clutter in our lives. From this work, I have built a foundation of clearing hacks to help you get back on track and focused on the great things that are happening in midlife.

You don't have to throw away everything but the kitchen sink. Your mission, should you choose to accept it, is to create order out of chaos and sift through things that have held you back emotionally, physically, professionally, and in every other area of your life. Once you learn how to let go, you will be weightless, free to fly off into the proverbial sunset and enjoy your life. And, at this stage of the game, you deserve that.

Here's to clearing the clutter and creating the space for you to ROCK your midlife season and beyond!

PS: I have a special gift for you, and it is FREE!

INTRODUCTION

The **30 Day Love your Home Decluttering Challenge** at www.loveyourhomedeclutteringchallenge.com will help you take action on the principles you read in this book, with 30 days of email prompts to help you tackle the clutter in your home.

As well, you'll receive a complimentary ebook when you register, along with another surprise along the way. Declutter your entire home in 30 days or collect the prompts and go at your own speed.

It's my gift to help you get started on your decluttering adventure!

Start your own 30 Day Love your Home Decluttering Challenge at this link:
www.loveyourhomedeclutteringchallenge.com

Finally, for tips, interviews and all things midlife - including decluttering, life reinvention, side hustles and more, tune in to the **Rocking Midlife® Podcast!**
https://catcoluccio.com/podcast

1

CLUTTER—THE NEMESIS TO YOUR BEST LIFE!

I'd like you to meet Laura. She's a 48-year-old, married mother of three teenagers. She spends most of her day juggling sports and school runs (when she can locate her keys), housework, a husband (who feels more like a roommate), a demanding boss, and aging parents moving into specialized care. She is overbooked and can't get a grip on the piles of dirty clothes and linen that multiply and divide in the laundry room. So much laundry! She often thinks to herself, *If I can just get organized,* not realizing that organizing stuff and actually decluttering your life are very different things.

Clutter, left unchecked, has the potential to seriously negatively impact every area of your life. We don't just store clutter in our homes. It shows up in our work environments, on our digital devices, and on our daily calendars. Excessive clutter is the nemesis to living your best life.

SKELETONS

A recurring scene in television cartoons and comedy sketches is one in which an unsuspecting stoic character opens a closet door to retrieve something and is met with an explosion of old junk. Beach balls, boxing gloves, magazines, worn-out shoes, and everything else in the closet topples onto his head. The poor guy just stands there in shock as he is assaulted by the deluge of miscellaneous mess escaping its cramped quarters.

If I were a character in that scenario, I would probably have been the person who shoved everything into that closet. As a recovering clutter-holic, I know firsthand how it feels to be overwhelmed by the myriad tasks and duties that never seem to get done. I've been a homeschooling parent, sports mom, chief cook, cleaner, chauffeur, spouse, and family administrator. I have launched several businesses, been a professional musician, and dabbled in various artistic pursuits, and I continue to have a passion for learning and trying new things. As a result, I've struggled continuously with endless laundry, overbooked schedules, work-life balance, and emotional fatigue. My skeletons were falling out of my closet and onto my own head. I learned the hard way how the disarray in our lives impacts productivity, creativity, morale, health, and wellness, especially in midlife when there are already so many other naturally occurring changes happening.

Clutter isn't just about the material things that fall out of your closet or the massive amounts of paperwork collecting dust on the kitchen table. While all of that can make you feel exhausted and overwhelmed, there is more to the rising tide of disorder in our lives than meets the eye. Speaker and professional organizer Kerry Thomas shared, "My life looked great and I was getting a lot of compliments, but I felt stuck. Why? I had massive amounts of emotional clutter" (Stillman, 2021). No matter how clean and organized your home is, a messy mind can also make you feel inadequate and stressed. Thomas says the below types of clutter can wreak havoc on your peace of mind (Stillman, 2021):

- **Physical:** overflowing closets, garages, and storage units
- **Digital:** unread emails, files saved on your computer, and any other digital paraphernalia
- **Mental:** anxiety, worry, and fear
- **Emotional:** negative patterns, beliefs, and lies you've told yourself about what you can and cannot do
- **Spiritual:** a lack of forgiveness and peace of mind

My life once included all of the above. My two children, a son and daughter, were elite athletes. My husband and I chose homeschooling in order to allow them the opportunity to travel the world and compete. Homeschooling often gets a bad rap. Most people think it means keeping your kids in the house and unsocialized all day every day. The truth is far from it. I was the learning coach and head parent in charge of de-escalation. I read papers, reviewed curriculums, and made sure their education was engaging and relevant. I was the liaison connecting them with mentors, trainers, physicians, and other educators and facilitators. There were piles of paperwork and a multitude of activities. As teenagers, the kids had plenty of friends, so there were still parties and events to attend, chaperone, and supervise. I was the resident taxi driver, laundress, teacher, trainer, accountant, scheduler, and deliverer of all things edible. I enjoyed the process, but there were days when I thought my head would explode trying to get through the neverending lists of things to do and places to be.

You don't have to be a homeschooling mom to feel this pressure. If you've got kids in school or at home, you know what I'm talking about. Or maybe you've got a partner who acts like a kid. Perhaps you're single and overwhelmed with work even though you love your job. The truth is, no one is coming in a cape to rescue you. However, there is hope, and you don't have to be a superwoman to break down the dynamic forces of your personal dastardly disorder. My own decluttering journey is a work in progress, and along the way, I've discovered the antidote to my clutter kryptonite. In my research to understand the impact of clutter on daily life, I built a foundation of clearing hacks to help you dust the pants off the skeletons in your closet.

THE EFFECTS OF CLUTTER ON SELF-PERCEPTION AND SELF-ESTEEM

Clutter affects everything from our decision-making processes to our diet and self-esteem. It includes the noise of negative thinking patterns, limiting beliefs, overanalyzing, and negative self-talk. Feelings of failure, shame, defeat, imposter syndrome, anxiety, and depression can be insidiously paralyzing. The lack of vulnerability and human connection can also clutter our minds to the point of emotional and spiritual overload.

Ask yourself why you feel the need to fill your life and mind with so much stuff. Storage units are a billion-dollar industry. When did we become such clutter vultures and why? All clutter comes from one major factor: a postponed decision. You throw the mail on the table and ignore it for a few days until it piles up and screams to be opened, answered, and discarded. The car suddenly stops and dies because you put off that oil change for tomorrow or next week, days when you bank on having more time. Fear drives you to the point of holding onto useless things. You don't step into your own light on the job even though you are uniquely qualified, because your mind is cluttered with all the stuff that could go wrong. You remember and stress out about a time 10 years ago when you made a choice that didn't go so well.

Guilt is emotional clutter. You're embarrassed by the things you haven't had time to clean or put in order. You don't ask for help when you know things have gotten out of hand, because you don't want to be judged or ridiculed. You don't have anyone over, and in the absence of human connection, you begin to surround yourself with things.

Hoarding, the excessive accumulation of material things, animals, and memorabilia causes a person to feel the need to save items whether or not those things have value. Anxiety and depression go hand in hand with this practice. The overwhelming need to keep everything can stem from rehashed hurts, bitterness, personality type, family dynamic, death of a loved one, or other significant losses. Symptoms usually occur between the ages of 11 and 15 and become increasingly difficult to address as you age. They include the following (Mayo Clinic Staff, 2018):

- Excessively acquiring unnecessary items until there's no space for them. This can include an overabundance of newspapers, books, magazines, clothing, paperwork, and sentimental items, as well as a buildup of food or trash to the point where it is unhealthy and unsanitary.
- Persistent difficulty and significant distress when throwing out or parting with things, regardless of actual value.
- The inability to keep yourself and others safe in your living environment. Clutter that causes a fire hazard, slips and falls, rodent and insect infestations, and copious other hazardous conditions make it more challenging to get medical or emergency assistance and can lead to loss of parental rights.
- Conflicts with others who try to help reduce or remove clutter from the home or workspace.
- Collecting things to the point where there isn't room for actual living. You can't cook in your kitchen, bathe in your bathroom, or sleep in your bedroom.
- Indecisiveness, perfectionism, avoidance, procrastination, and problems with planning and

organizing. These can lead to legal problems like eviction or other forced removal from the home.

The unfortunate results of this disorder include loneliness, social isolation, financial hardship, loss of personal and parental rights, depression, anxiety, and other stress disorders. Think about how you address your cluttered mind. What's going on inside our heads usually shows up in our home disguised as overabundance, confusion, and disorganization. Don't be fooled by how pristine your surroundings are. You can have a clean house and still have a *dirty* mind.

THE EFFECTS OF CLUTTER ON WORK AND PRODUCTIVITY

Postponing a decision is usually associated with fear. We avoid opening the mail because we fear bad news. We expect it. For various reasons, we prefer to bury our proverbial heads in the sand. Did you know ostriches don't really do that? Quite the opposite. An ostrich will chase you for miles if you ruffle its feathers, and sprinting at 45 miles per hour or more, they're extremely fast and ferocious birds. Unlike us, they prefer to deal with their issues head-on.

Mess equals stress. If you can't find something, especially if you need it immediately, the stress associated with the search can leave you feeling inadequate and disoriented. Coworkers and those in leadership positions may judge you incapable when you can't readily access what's needed. This can cost you the promotion or raise you deserve. While creatives tend to be messy, there is something to be said for finding peace and the papers you neatly filed away.

In our attempt to be impressive, we fool ourselves into believing we can multitask, but multitasking is a myth. Your brain is not designed to focus on several things at once. It has a way of short-circuiting when there is too much of anything. Moving papers around your desk or to the next room is not organizing; it's shifting. Generating copious to-do lists creates anxiety and does not effectively move the needle. You make sustainable progress when you are able to zero in on one task at a time. Focus moves you forward.

THE EFFECTS OF CLUTTER ON HEALTH AND WELLNESS

A cluttered mind can lead to accidents from preoccupation, inattentiveness, and sleep deprivation. Insomnia inhibits decision-making. In sleep, your brain powers down to sweep itself clean. Your tendency to zone out, difficulty comprehending, and faulty deductive reasoning are signs that your brain needs to be recharged. Sleep is the brain's download system that keeps your neurotransmitters healthy and firing at maximum speed.

Clutter creates stress. Stress causes elevated cortisone levels which generate the fight, flight, or freeze response. Constant stress can negatively impact your organs, including your heart and liver, causing heart attacks and autoimmune disease in the body. Did you know most heart attacks occur on Monday morning, between the hours of 4:00 and 10:00 a.m.? Saturday, the day you rush around trying to get a handle on all the tasks you weren't able to complete during the week, comes in second. Uncontrolled emotion, overexertion, and overeating are the leading causes of heart attacks in mature women (Thomas, 2009).

CHALLENGING MINIMALISM

World economies are built on our lust for more and better. Advertisements are aimed at our psychological need to be bigger, better, stronger, prettier, healthier, and sexier. These unrealistic needs are so ingrained in us that the older we get, the harder it is to let go of the need for material consumption. In the beginning, sorting and throwing out can be time-consuming, causing anxiety and stress—the very things we're trying to avoid. We play the what-if game, worrying about what will happen if we toss something that we end up needing later. But what if cleaning that closet made you feel like you could breathe again? What if freeing up more space internally and externally gave you some peace of mind? Think of all the possibilities.

Living a minimalist lifestyle is not about living in the woods and making homemade beef jerky. If that's what you want to do, go for it, but minimalism at its core is about living more simply. Purging becomes a lifestyle choice when you realize the accumulation of things isn't the prerequisite for peace of mind. Some major hurdles to becoming a minimalist are below (Brauer, 2016):

> **Purging never ends.** Initially, removing clutter is challenging and time-consuming, but once it becomes a habit, decluttering can be a joyous occasion, allowing you to be supportive, giving, productive, and financially stable.
>
> **You have to embrace letting go.** Deciding what to toss, donate, or keep can be difficult when you are emotionally attached or share possession of an item with someone. Things that have sentimental value are the hardest to let go. Below are some questions you can ask yourself:
>
> - What purpose is the item serving?
> - How often is it used?
> - Does it bring happiness?

It challenges you as a family. Everyone likes to receive gifts. Many of us enjoy shopping for something new. The communication of family desires, wants, and needs can come starkly into play when you're trying to downsize. Here are ways to address this challenge:

- Ask friends and family to give to a charitable organization for Christmas instead of giving gifts to you or your young children.
- Ask people what they need and give consumable gifts. Money is always useful.
- Use mindfulness and meditation to help you stay calm and free of mental clutter.
- Avoid the retail trap of enticing sales, glossy advertisements, beautiful store windows, and exotic displays. Ask yourself if you really need to buy the item and why.

Minimalism is about adding value to your life and discarding, repurposing, or donating things that don't give you peace, joy, and freedom. Clutter is a thief that steals your time, energy, space, money, relationships, and independence. The negative effects of excess can include (Simple Lionheart Life, 2019)

- discontentment
- negative impact on mental health
- interference with physical health
- loss of freedom from a lifestyle that ties you to what you own
- decreased productivity due to distraction and overstimulation
- loss of peace because of overwhelming chaos and frustration

- negative impact on overall well-being and quality of life

Decluttering helps you gain control of your environment, clear mental space, and open doors to a fuller, healthier, richer, happier life. It doesn't mean you have to live in a cave. It is not determined by whether you are rich, poor, or middle class. You can discover the joy of practicing minimalism whether you live in a cottage or a mansion. It may be a challenge initially, but the benefits far outweigh the obstacles. Once you discover what matters most to you, decluttering can be a means to developing a more empowering vision for your life.

2

WHAT MATTERS TO YOU?

It's one thing to say you don't want a cluttered life, but what *do* you want? When Laura dreams of a decluttered life, she envisions empty laundry baskets and a pristine kitchen. There are no urgent emails to answer or notifications from her boss. She is contentedly spending an evening with her husband, a glass of wine in hand and a romantic comedy streaming on television.

Laura's husband has dreams too. His perfect day involves a garage where he can locate all of his tools without having to dig through the children's sports gear and a weekend to himself with no appointments.

Visualization is an important part of the journey to decluttering your space, but how do you create a cohesive vision when you have a family and everyone has different ideas of minimalism, simplification, and organization? How do you define the parameters? What are the boundaries? Johnny loves his old fuzzy teddy bear, but Mom knows the germ-filled creature needs to be trashed. Dad thinks Mom's fabric scraps are trash. Mom thinks the golf clubs he hasn't used in 10 years should be sold online. Communication is the only way to know what really matters to you and your family.

VISUALIZATION: YOUR SECRET SAUCE

Wouldn't it be great to have a crystal ball and see into the future or superpowers and decide the future for you and your family? How would that change your life?

There is a saying that "a battle is won twice—first in mind and second in reality" (Rao Ph.D., 2020). I don't have a crystal ball, but I do know that visualization can help you realize your goals. When you can control the thousands of thoughts that run through your mind every day and focus only on a few things, you can order your life in a way that benefits you and those you love and care for. Research shows visualization includes several benefits, as seen below (Rao Ph.D., 2020):

- It eliminates bad habits and builds good ones.
- It helps you dream big and achieve greater success.
- It rewires your connections by aligning your outside world with your inside world.
- It develops internal focus of control to make things fall into place.
- It reorients your conscious and subconscious thought processes.
- It eliminates distraction.
- It enhances concentration.
- It strengthens your subconscious mind and internal motivation.

There's evidently a great deal of value in setting aside time each day to imagine your ideal environment. What does that look like for you? Engage your five senses to create a picture of your perfect space. What colors do you see? Are the fabrics in the room soft, furry, or leathery? What aromas fill the rooms? Are the furnishings modern, contemporary, or classic? Does the kitchen have shells, closets, an electric trash can, a gourmet cooking stove? Is your bathroom a spa oasis? Be as imaginatively detailed as possible. You've got to see it in your mind's eye before you can ever see it in real life.

Write what you see. Writing it down helps your brain sharpen your vision and find ways to fulfill it. The more senses you use, the more the brain can laser in on what it takes to achieve the dream.

Our brains operate through repetition. We learned to walk, talk, read, do math, and eat by repetitive movement and practice. There are days you drive yourself to the job without thinking about where you're going. Your brain, on autopilot, gets there whether you remember the driving experience or not. Writing your goals and reading them first thing in the morning and last thing at night trains your brain to accomplish miracles. With continual input and action, your brain's brilliance can make your dream a reality.

Success and failure are largely dependent on mindset. Where your mind goes, everything else follows. Your habits, self-esteem, character, and the way in which you live your life are dependent upon what you are feeding yourself mentally. Visualization is the key to the kingdom. You have to see it and believe it before you can get anywhere close to making something a reality.

MINIMALIST, SIMPLIFIED, OR ORGANIZED

Minimalism, simplification, and organization are often used interchangeably and, as such, can be very confusing. Let's break it down.

By definition, *minimalism* is about reducing your carbon footprint, recycling, reusing, or discarding. It is about living with intention, clarity, and peace of mind. *Simplification* implies breaking things down to the basic essentials. It's the term used in math equations relating to reducing things to their lowest common denominator. Do you need all 15 of those suits, or will fewer do?

How many shoes do you really need? How many cars can you drive at a time? Can you live without half your stuff? *Organization* refers to a methodical system of order. Everything has a place, and everything is in its prescribed place. All of these terms are subjective. You can use any one of them to describe your end goal. When you understand what it is you're aiming for, you'll know when you've reached your destination and when to celebrate the journey.

Once you have visualized the goal for your personal space, it's time to communicate that vision to your family and others who may be affected by the changes you would like to make. Knowing how to explain the subtle differences between minimalism, simplification, and organization will help you to create a clearer vision for others to support. Communication is essential in order to get a thorough understanding of what works best for everyone. Some people seem to work well in organized chaos while others are totally thrown off balance by any type of clutter. You can be organized and not neat or neat and not organized. You can be a minimalist when it comes to furniture but be a clothes hoarder or a paper fiend. Knowing what works for you and the people around you will sharpen the vision and motivate a team effort.

While you may be able to do some things as a solo act, many bigger projects will require a crew. You need to be in tune with everyone on the team in order for things to go smoothly. It's never a good idea to force others to change in a way they don't feel is beneficial to them. Your family may not be interested in making do with less, and that's okay. Do what you can. What clutter of your own can you get in order, and what kind of order are you looking for? On the job, you may aim for better organization of your desk or personal filing system. You might want to simplify your storage facility and minimize what you shop for. You may opt for more quiet meditative time to get your thoughts in order or decide on a weight loss program to feel healthier.

No matter what terms you use to define it, decluttering is all about opening yourself up to more space physically, mentally, and emotionally. It's about giving yourself the opportunity to have more freedom, greater productivity, and increased time. If you want to sell others on the idea of downsizing, find out how it benefits them and sell them on that.

HOARDERS IN REAL TIME

Do you have a compulsive need to keep everything? Do you feel heightened anxiety when you throw anything out? A married woman in her forties, we'll call her Stephanie, lost her husband to a debilitating disease. Although she had kept her house basically clean, she began to collect and keep things. Over time, those things became clutter that weighed down her house. Old rusted canned goods sat in a cabinet on shelves curling from the weight. New cans were added on a weekly basis, yet the old rusted ones remained. The refrigerator was filled with plastic containers of moldy meatloaf, fruit, or mystery meals. Papers, books, mail, old newspapers, street signs, and advertisements were strewn across the dining room and completely covered the beautiful cherry wood table. People had long since stopped visiting and calling. This didn't matter to Stephanie. She had no desire for company. She preferred to sit alone in her lounge chair staring out the window, cursing passersby, and watching television as dust gathered like thick clumps of dough on windowsills and furniture. This is an example of what hoarding looks like.

We all collect stuff we don't need. Some of it we hold onto even though it has no value to us. Who doesn't have a junk drawer in their kitchen? Maybe yours is in your office, a hall closet, the garage, or the basement. What treasures would we find in the abyss of your storage unit?

This penchant for collecting things, however, can go far beyond the normal scope. In 2007, Lorraine Brennan lived with her father, son, and fiance in Massachusetts. Brennan was a compulsive hoarder. She and her intended husband had been engaged for eight years. He couldn't bring himself to carry through with the marriage because, after living with her for quite some time, he couldn't accept her compulsive buying and holding onto things. Their house was so cluttered, Brennan's son was too embarrassed to invite kids over from school. The couple's bedroom, which doubled as an office, was stuffed to bursting with odds and ends collected over a long period of time. Brennan despaired that her husband-to-be would leave her before ever getting to the altar (Bouchardeau and Delarosa, 2008).

Janie Allocca also had a hoarding problem. Her house was so filled with clutter that it was unlivable. She couldn't get to her kitchen or sit on any furniture. Her house was so jam-packed with stuff, she lived among the piles until, eventually, she used the entire two-story family home as a storage facility and went to live with her mother.

Someone suffering from a compulsive hoarder disorder, often associated with obsessive-compulsive disorder, the mental process of choosing to throw something away is psychologically painful. Dr. David Tolin, director of the Anxiety Disorders Center at the Institute of Living in Hartford, Connecticut, explains hoarding:

> The person who hoards is going through a very, very effortful search of their memory to try to think of as many things as they can about this item before they make the decision. What this all amounts to then is a painful and effortful process of decision making, that you and I might take for granted (Bouchardeau & Delarosa, 2008).

There is no medicinal cure for compulsive hoarder disorder but there is hope. Progress has been made in the area of cognitive behavioral therapy (CBT), which can include non-acquiring or nonshopping therapy, clutter workshops, and support groups. Allocca said, after being involved in therapy, she can "actually see the mess. I can acknowledge and accept that I have this problem" (Bouchardeau & Delarosa, 2008). Before therapy, she lived in a massive hodgepodge of disorder, chaos, and rubbish. To others, the jumbled mess was evident. To her, it was normal. She still struggles with stress, bad habits, and avoidance, but because she is more aware of the problem, she has been able to make significant progress.

Although these hoarder horror stories are extreme cases, they demonstrate the real conflicts involved in decluttering and what that means to you and your family. When your stuff crowds your life, everyone is affected. Letting go is never easy. There is an emotional component to it. Whether you are watching your children leave the nest and go off to college, you're divorcing a spouse, have just become a widow, or are happily married but trying to recapture the hopeful dreams of your youth, all kinds of feelings will arise. Letting go takes time and practice, but once you get out from under the rubble, you will free yourself, your family, and others around you. When you clean up, clear out, sort, tidy, and straighten, you create liberty and freedom for all.

3

PHYSICAL CLUTTER—A WALK THROUGH YOUR BEDROOMS, BATHROOMS, ENTRY, AND LIVING AREAS

Physical clutter in the home has the ability to create a frenzy in day-to-day living. Consider how much time Laura may have spent on a regular basis trying to locate her keys, find a misplaced electric bill, or discover there was no dog food for Bowser right at feeding time! Imagine what happens if, when she finds the electric bill, it's overdue and mildewed. Now she's got to negotiate and come up with additional resources. Bowser has just snatched little Timmy's favorite cookie out of his hand. Timmy is screaming and chasing the dog through the house. All of this, and she just got home from a crazy day at work!

Home may be where the heart is, but clutter in the home can give you a heart attack, literally and figuratively. With that in mind, household clutter is your first area of conquest.

CELEBRATE SMALL WINS

Let's start with a celebration. I know that sounds crazy. After all, what's there to celebrate when the laundry is piled up to the ceiling? I want to challenge you to think about how often you go from one task to the next without celebrating what you've already accomplished. We are programmed to work nonstop without giving ourselves credit for completed tasks. We are not encouraged to celebrate small wins but instead to do more and more to the point of exhaustion. The "I can sleep when I die" mentality pushes us into constant movement at the expense of our health and well-being. So, before we begin addressing your physical clutter, let's start by celebrating what's good.

What efforts are you making at self-care? Is there something you do right now that gives you pleasure and brings you peace? What parts of your life are free of clutter? Do you exercise at least twice a week, and by exercise, I mean anything that gives you energy. This can include walking around the block, gardening, or dancing to your favorite song. Are you able to get to work on time most, if not all, of the time? Celebrate. Do you manage to get the kids up and out in time for school? Celebrate. Are you a parent with more than one child? Celebrate a few times if you haven't yet lost your sanity. The point is to find the prize in the Cracker Jack box of your chaos. When you do, pat yourself on the back and give yourself a hand.

The fact that you have begun this journey means that you are winning. The first steps are always the most challenging. Watch any toddler learning to walk, and you'll see that small wins add up. Don't count yourself out when you fall or falter. Don't overwhelm yourself by taking on too much at one time or being so extreme in your cutting back that, in panic, you run out and buy more stuff. Every little bit you can do counts, so don't count yourself out.

ENERGY AND MOTIVATION

You've got your visual. You have determined what minimizing looks and feels like to you and your family. You've celebrated what you have already accomplished in your life that attributes to clarity and success. But all you see around you is a mess. How do you get motivated, and what strategies do you use to get started? If you're physically challenged, where will you find the energy? If you work a lot, how will you find the time? Here are a few simple steps to follow:

- **Break it down.** Start with a small area and follow through until you get it done. It doesn't have to be the entire closet. Pick a shelf. Organize your shoes. Choose five or ten things to donate and donate them immediately. Baby steps.
- **Set a timer.** Do you have thirty seconds? A minute? Thirty minutes? Make a game of it and see how much you can get done in the time you set.
- **Create a team.** For larger projects, get together with friends and family. Use the game method. Be creative and have fun with it. Set your timer and see which team completes their assigned task first. Offer silly prizes. Enjoy the process.
- **Hype it up!** Music generates energy. Find a tune that motivates you to operate at peak performance. Dance or whistle as you work. Upbeat instrumentals like percussion, piano, and violin create focus and intensity.
- **Celebrate to motivate.** Once you've completed a task, give yourself a reward. Relax with a glass of wine for five minutes. Do focused breathing for ten. Whatever works for you. Then, take that energy into the next thing.

Motivation and energy are about movement. If you visualize your goals, get them down in words and pictures and add action to them. You will be amazed at how much you can accomplish, even when you are taking baby steps.

THE INNER SANCTUM

The bedroom and the bathroom are the most private spaces in your home. They both have closed-door policies. Only solo and specified guests are allowed. Your bedroom is your inner sanctum, or at least it should be.

Most of us who experience sleep deprivation can attribute it, in large part, to clutter in our bedrooms. From over burgeoning closets to dust bunnies and layers of shoes under the bed, clutter can cause anxiety that results in sleepless nights. You may lay your head on the pillow and close your eyes, but sleep eludes you when your mind is filled with tasks left undone. Poor sleep hygiene can make you grumpy and out of sorts in the morning. Copious cups of coffee cannot recover sleep.

The bedroom wasn't always the private niche we know it as today. Centuries ago, before privacy was the norm, bedrooms were communal. People lived, worked, and slept in the same spaces together. Great rooms housed large fireplaces to cook on and to keep everyone warm on cold nights. Private bedrooms didn't come about until the 15th and 16th centuries. These rooms, always positioned on the upper floors, were the VIP section for the elite. Today, the bedroom still gets VIP status.

Bedroom furnishings were also vastly different from today's version. The ancients slept on grass, animal fur, and straw. The term *hit the hay* is derived from the ancient tradition of stuffing a hemp sack with bunches of hay to sleep on. Slabs of rock were also used. The earliest known bedding was created by the ancient people of Sibudu, South Africa, over 77,000 years ago. In China, during the Neolithic period about 7,200 years ago, people heated stone platforms to sleep on. Both forms of bedding are still in existence today. In Rome, beds weren't restricted to one room, but used everywhere in the home. The ancient Egyptians are responsible for the form we recognize as a bed today, complete with a head and footboard (Reagan, 2015).

The bedroom as the inner sanctum can be attributable to the fact that births and deaths took place in the bedrooms of the wealthy and middle class. Children were born and raised there. Elaborate beds were created for the upper class who were passing away, thus the term *death bed*. In 1714, England's Queen Anne designed a very elaborate bed with five mattresses for her deathbed. It also featured ornately embroidered coverings, valences, and drapings (Reagan, 2015).

Today, beds are wonderful, comfortable things with pillow top mattresses, sleep numbers, and adjustability for back pain and other ailments. The bedchamber of old, with its many rooms and enough space per square foot for kings and queens to hold court, has dramatically changed. As the power of the monarchy dwindled, so did the bedrooms, especially in middle class homes. By the 19th century, there were separate bedrooms for children. Bedroom designs and functionality changed drastically through the years as revolutionary technologies made things less expensive for the general population. Bedroom luxuries now include blackout curtains, special lighting, spacious closets, luxurious ensuites, thickly carpeted or heated floors, and soundproof walls. Thanks to modern marketing, there's more stuff than ever in a lot less space. Your challenge, should you choose to accept it, is to clean and clear the space. A perfect sleep number on your bed won't help you catch any zzzz's if clutter abounds.

Your first area of attack is very simple. Start by making your bed in the morning. This task is actually a part of basic military training. It increases mental discipline and daily motivation, and it gives you a sense of accomplishment. We are creatures of habit. Making the bed puts you in the habit of clearing your mind of everything that went on the day before. It gives you a sense of starting over, starting something new. A freshly made bed motivates you to do more, and there's nothing like coming home and being able to fall into it at night. These small wins will help you to focus on the day ahead and get a good night's sleep.

Inventory your bedroom furniture. What's working? What's just taking up space? An upholstered bench can be used as a sitting space, as well as a place for storing linen or clothing. Shrink-wrap style plastic bags increase space. A clothes hamper with a lid can do double duty as decorative furniture and overflow prevention. Embellished boxes purchased at your local discount store can house small objects. You can also recycle a shoebox by trimming it with fabric or contact paper.

Before you buy anything new, take stock of what you have. Eliminate what's not working. Toss out broken things you haven't taken the time or been inclined to fix. Donate or sell functional pieces that are just gathering dust. Once you've finished, you will more clearly see the possible vision for this space. Begin decluttering with baby steps. Start with a small space, like the top of your dresser, nightstand, or ensuite counter. Following are a few suggestions:

- Get rid of earrings with no matches, broken jewelry, and stuff you don't wear or want. Use the toss or donate method at least once a month.
- Place lotions and potions on a decorative tray. Toss empty and expired bottles.
- Separate hair, skin, and nail products by using small square plastic or wire baskets you can purchase at your local discount store.
- Clear your nightstand of everything except the essentials: reading glasses, a bottle of water, and your journal or a good book.
- Keep items beside your bed below eye level. The less you have to focus on, the better.

The space under the bed is just as important as what's on and around the bed. Under-the-bed clutter can make you feel restless during the night and interrupt sleep. If you absolutely need to use this area, pack away seasonal things you won't be using for a while in flat storage containers and shrink-wrap plastic.

Closets, once used more for prayer, contemplation, and reflection than for clothing, are much bigger fish to fry. Back in the day, coming out the closet had to do with entering the world spiritually clothed. Today, closets are the most coveted space in any home and the biggest clutter culprits in any room, especially the bedroom. Unworn clothing, shoes, and accessories overflow in unholy matrimony, increasing your anxiety and frustration on a regular basis. Your own temper tantrums and screaming rants do nothing to motivate you to change this nightmare of epic proportions.

You will never get what you want if you can't see it and don't know why you want it. When it comes to closets, a good place to start is mapping out your vision. Closetsbydesign.com has hundreds of ideas for walk-in and reach-in closets, as well as office and bedroom spaces. Discover the ideal design for you. Ask yourself why you want the shelf to look that way or the hamper to sit there. Your why fuels your vision. Map everything out with drawings, printouts, and pictures.

Once you've visualized the goal, you can begin decluttering accordingly. Keep in mind that decluttering is about releasing. When you toss, donate, sell, or keep an item, you are making a judgment about what matters in your life. Worn, frazzled items represent your past emotional baggage. Let them go. Items that no longer fit or suit your current style do not represent who you are in the present. Be honest with yourself. Forget all your New Year's resolutions. Live in the present moment. Release the guilt and depression that comes with "if only" and "I remember when." Keep only what serves you right now. Once you release your past, you can live in the present and create a new future.

Select one small section at the top, middle, or bottom of your closet. Set a timer for 30 minutes. Break those 30 minutes down into 10-minute segments. The space you choose should be manageable within your specified time frame. This will keep you from getting discouraged and, if you're anything like most of us, from wreaking havoc by pulling out everything at once. Get some music going from your playlist, turn up the volume, and begin.

Make three piles: one for things you're going to toss, another for things you're going to keep, and a third for things you will sell or donate. Working only in your chosen section, take ten minutes to place things in the toss, donate, or keep piles. Don't spend too much time thinking about it. Touch an item for three seconds, and then put it in the place that feels right. Toss out those things that are too shabby to be useful. Use a trash bag for tossing so you don't get tempted to store those old rags, beat-up shoes, or frazzled hats. Let them go! Set aside those things you are going to keep. You will put these things back in place after the space you've chosen has been completely cleared. Toss the things you are going to donate in a plastic bin. Don't worry about being neat. The object of the game is to be quick and not overthink the process.

When you have finished tossing things, immediately take the trash out, so you won't be tempted to dig up your past again. Sort through those items you are going to keep. If you haven't worn it in the last two seasons, place it in the donation pile. Separate your seasonal items. If it's summer, place winter clothes in clear storage containers, and vice versa. Use shrink-wrap bags to fit more items neatly. If you have entrepreneurial interests, gather together those gently used items you would like to sell, and then check out websites like Poshmark, thredUP, Pinterest, and eBay to sell your clothing online. You could also look into local consignment shops. Take donated items to your nearest women's or men's shelter, Red Cross, or Purple Heart. Make a plan to drop them off before or after work, or during your regular errand run. Prior planning leads to greater success.

Some additional things to consider to help you get more room out of your closet space are below (Larkin, 2022):

- Change your hangers. Soft, velvety hangers hold fabric in place and help clothing items keep their shape. Tiered hangers can be used to increase space. Avoid using wire hangers which tangle in other hangers and cause clutter.
- Organize your clothing by length. Arrange shirts with shirts, skirts with skirts, dresses with dresses, and slacks with slacks. This creates more space on the closet floor for shoes.
- Use over-the-door hook racks for lightweight items like hats, scarves, and other accessories. Make sure not to overburden a door as it will loosen the hinges and cause the door to fall. You're not trying to create more problems for yourself.
- Use layered shoe racks or other shoe organizers that can hang on a door or over a closet bar.
- Use clear storage boxes or shelf dividers to maximize shelf space. Your folded sweaters, sweatshirts, and other bulky items can go in these storage boxes or stay neat with a shelf divider.

Get in the habit of releasing things at least once a week. If you buy something new, let go of something you no longer use. If you like the idea of entrepreneurship but know you're not organized and committed enough to do an online clothing business, release the items instead. If you plan to start an entrepreneurial venture, don't be afraid to ask for help. Set yourself up to win.

Once you've experienced the dopamine thrill of success, you can choose another space to clean and clear. You don't have to do it all in one day. Commit to a regular decluttering sweep once a week for 30 minutes and record your progress. Be sure to include in your journal how you felt once your space was cleared. This will keep you motivated on days when you don't feel like doing anything. Make sure to celebrate your accomplishments.

THE ROYAL FLUSH

The bathroom is the most traversed area in the home. Whether it's Mom and Dad's ensuite, the general bathroom, or the powder room, the bathroom is in use more times a day than any room in the house. Not only do people practically live there, it's also home to copious germs and bacteria, those little nuisances that can make a whole lot of people sick. A clean, sanitized, orderly bathroom can have an impact on the overall health and well-being of everyone in the house, including guests. Cleanliness and organization are key. Nobody wants to be missing toilet tissue at an inopportune moment. And who wants the blind search for a clean towel when shampoo is burning your retina?

The bathroom is where we keep all those products that we hope will make us flawless. We spend hundreds, even thousands of dollars on beauty products and feel guilty about throwing them away when they don't work. Free samples of hair and skin products, travel toiletries pilfered from hotel rooms, and makeup that isn't in our color palette fill cabinets and drawers. Empty packages, bottles, opened containers, and half-used products line the shelves. Eyelash curlers, rusty tweezers, worn fingernail files, dried up nail polish, expired shaving cream, and other lotions and potions can be found inside shower stalls, scattered around the tub, in windowsills, and anywhere else there is space. Clearing can be extremely stressful, but not doing it can be toxic as the overwhelm continually adds to our guilt and shame.

Having an emotional attachment to these things can also make it difficult for you to discard things. You may have received lotions, bath salts, and perfumes as gifts and feel bad about getting rid of them, even though you don't like or use them. You may have become attached to products you've spent a great deal of money purchasing because you don't want to feel wasteful. Vitamins are another expensive purchase. We buy into the fantasy that if we buy this wig, take this vitamin, use this lotion or perfume, we'll be more attractive to everyone, we'll have no more problems, and the world will be sunshine and roses. There is no magic potion for self-esteem. Forgive yourself for the money you spent, accept the lesson, trash the useless product, and move on.

When cleaning, consider that you are releasing the garbage in your life. More stuff in the bathroom equals more germs. For sanitary reasons, things like old toothbrushes, used or old cotton balls, worn out makeup brushes, sponges, and tissues should all go into the garbage immediately. Discard mousse, wigs, and extensions you no longer use. Check expiration dates on all medications, including over the counter and supplements. Toss outdated items. Work with bite-sized piles at a time in quick ten-minute increments. Hold the item you're considering for three seconds or less, make your peace with it, then dump it either in the garbage, your keep pile, or a box for donating. Hair tools like flat irons, curling irons, hair dryers, and other such gadgets in good condition that you don't use would be welcome at a women's shelter. Make sure these items are in working order and chords are safe and intact.

Ripped towels can be recycled as cleaning rags for your car. Trash overused washcloths. Place anything you're going to keep neatly in a small container that you can sort through later. Keep in mind that you're not just getting rid of things you have no use for; you're getting rid of guilt, shame, and negative energy. How does that feel?

When it comes to organizing, here are a few ideas to consider (Carlson, 2016):

- Keep your daily makeup in a makeup pouch in your purse. Weekend or special makeup can go into a separate container you keep in your linen closet or dresser drawer.
- Store makeup brushes and toothbrushes in mason jars.
- Keep only what you need and use every day in the bathroom. Store any excess in a linen closet in containers.
- Keep medical emergency supplies like Band-Aids, Neosporin, anti-bacterial agents, and other necessities in a container in the linen closet.
- Attach a file organizer to your sink or inside a cabinet door to hold your hair dryer, hair curlers, flatirons, and other such equipment.
- Create a shelf over the door for supplies you don't use every day. This can include your special occasion makeup, extra cotton balls and other lightweight supplies, and first aid items.
- Use a kitchen tray organizer to keep bathroom drawers neat.
- Make use of plastic containers to separate cleaning products and other items to keep them organized and ready to use.
- Check out your local Container Store for other bathroom storage ideas.

Decluttering your bathroom is about protecting your self-image. It's about having more self-esteem and being able to look in the mirror and love who you are without the ghosts of failures past screaming at you from the cabinets.

ENTRYWAYS AND LIVING SPACES

The living room is the space where life happens. Toys creep out of the bedroom to hide under living room furniture or be trampled underfoot. Food and drinks skip the dining room and land on a coffee table—or under one. Bookbags, tennis shoes, a grandchild's chewed up morsel, dog biscuits, spills, stray homework, newspapers, books, and magazines all find a place in the living room and entryway. When you look around at the clutter it's easy to wonder how you got there.

Every home, like every person, comes with baggage. The paraphernalia we pick up in our day-to-day living accumulates and crowds out space. This area needs a clean sweep, and having a team goes a long way to getting the task completed. Gather your family, turn on some music, and have everyone pick a corner to start. Set up your toss, donate, and keep bins. Clear the floor first. A clean floor creates space and makes you feel accomplished. Use your timer, throw things in the proper baskets for a score, or see who can get things back to their rooms the fastest. I know you're not one of the seven dwarfs, but whistling while you work wouldn't hurt. Make it fun!

Good Housekeeping offers a few tips on decluttering your living space (Hines, 2019):

- Don't keep large exercise equipment in your living room.
- Keep the pretty pillows to a minimum. Lots of cushions, especially those that have you sitting on the edge of your seat, are impractical. They should be accents, not the whole shebang.
- Create a command station in the kitchen or entryway with stackable trays for incoming and outgoing mail. Touch your mail once and either file it, trash it, or answer it accordingly. Don't touch the mail until you are

- ready to deal with its contents. That way you don't track it through the house.
- Keep ironing and laundry in the laundry room. If you live in an apartment that doesn't have a laundry room, keep it in a storage closet. Put laundry away as soon as it's done so you don't have to look at it piling up day after day. Teach your children to fluff, fold, and iron their own so that the entire task doesn't fall on you.
- Sell or donate digital clutter including old DVDs, VHS videos, and other audio, visual, technological, or literary items you no longer use.
- Purge magazines you've already read each month. Magazine racks are clutter collectors for out-of-date magazines.
- Use cubbies or other decorative functional furnishings if you have to store things for your tiny tots in the living room. Ensure your children have adequate toy and equipment storage in their bedrooms.
- Opt for furniture with storage, like ottomans and coffee tables. Use dividers in drawers to keep them neat. Steer clear of oversized furniture if the square footage of your home doesn't allow for it. This is both a space and safety issue.
- Avoid creating a dusty knick-knack haven with endless ornaments, keepsakes, and collectibles on display.

As you are collecting and clearing items, ask yourself if that particular item would be more functional somewhere else. Give yourself three seconds to touch and release as you did in your bathroom. What emotions come up when you touch a particular item? Is it a negative or positive memory? The more negativity you can release from the space, the clearer your thinking will become and the more positive you will feel.

An entryway that is inviting and functional is an introduction to your home and who you are. Keep decor to a minimum. Fewer things equal fewer dust collectors. Use hooks and shelves for hanging coats, hats, scarves, and bookbags. Create a drop zone for boots and umbrellas by leaving a crate or cubby at the front door. Make entryways inviting by adding two or three decorative pieces grouped together, an assortment of books, and pretty bowls to keep car and house keys. Keep it simple.

Take advantage of the 10-minute cleanup in your living room when you have guests arriving on short notice. If you have a place for everything, it's much easier to put it in its place than to find a place for it. The 10-minute rule is your measuring stick. If you can't make the area presentable in 10 minutes, it's time to declutter and reorganize.

Letting go can be difficult at best, strenuous and immobilizing at worst. Take a moment to gauge how you're feeling now that you've decluttered these vital spaces in your home. What emotions came up for you as you cleaned? What emotions surfaced after you were done? How has this exercise helped you physically, emotionally, spiritually? Jot the answers to these questions down in your journal.

Clutter is loud, and like a sonic boom, it explodes into our lives causing us mental stress. When you clear your physical space, you let in air and light both externally and internally. This leads to better physical and mental health, personal growth, and motivation. Below are some other aftereffects of minimizing and organizing (Combiths, 2015):

- **Healing from the past.** Some of our physical possessions are actually triggers, bringing up old memories and flashbacks of painful times in our lives. Letting go can be painful but cathartic. The triumph is in allowing yourself to feel free of the hold that item had on you by discarding it.
- **Empowerment and self-control.** Making decisions about what to keep and what to let go of or give away strengthens you to make more difficult decisions. You gain a sense of control over yourself and your environment. You begin to believe you can take that next step and do that next thing you've been putting off in your life. Your confidence and positive self-perception increases.
- **A sense of freedom.** Each thing that leaves your house, whether as trash, donations, or gifts, is one less thing you have to keep track of, organize, and clean. You've bought yourself more time to do what you enjoy and to be more present for those you love.

Overcrowded living spaces can leave you feeling claustrophobic, anxious, and depressed. The more crowded your outward space, the more congested your thoughts. "Our physical environments significantly influence our cognition, emotions, and subsequent behaviors, including our relationships with others" (Sander, 2019). If we want to live our best lives, we have to clear out what's closing in on us.

4

PHYSICAL CLUTTER—A WALK THROUGH YOUR KITCHEN, LAUNDRY ROOM, AND GARAGE

You are finally getting enough sleep to be able to cope and even feel refreshed in the morning. Your bedroom is now the place of refuge, the sweet inner chamber, the real VIP section you always wanted it to be. You can take a royal flush in the bathroom without being assaulted by miscellaneous lotions, potions, and sticky substances. When you walk through your front door, you are no longer assailed by piles of laundry in the living room. You're not tripping over toys or stressing over months-old stacks of junk mail. You are at ease in these spaces. You can breathe. Pat yourself on the back for a job well done, but don't take your foot off the gas just yet. You are about to enter the drop zone.

I know you want to run back to your nice, newly organized bedroom and hide under the covers. I can hear your teeth chattering and your knees knocking. In midlife, it might sound more like the creaking of an old staircase. No worries! Hiding won't be necessary. The trepidation when it comes to tackling the kitchen, laundry, and garage is to be expected. You can bring these areas under submission using the same previous methods, so get your vision book and let's begin.

THE DROP ZONE

Does everyone in your home drop things wherever they fall when they come into the house? Do abandoned bookbags, loose homework papers, craft projects, coupons, and other miscellaneous items greet you on the kitchen counter, the floor, or anywhere there is space? The kitchen, otherwise known as the heart of the home, is one of the primary places where clutter abounds. It's the first place hungry children run when they get in from school or a sporting event. The refrigerator is practically a revolving door of greedy hands searching for something edible. The kitchen table is where plans for the day begin and discussions of who did what to whom at work or at school take place. It's where both the heart and the body find nourishment. Homemade soup like momma used to make on cold winter nights, cookies like grandma's, and your parents' hugs and kisses all happen in the kitchen.

What also happens is an assorted gathering of kids' drawings, bills, school notices, cell phone cords, comic books, coupons, and a miscellaneous hodgepodge of items that appear like ghosts gliding in from parts unknown. I wondered, for example, why in the world there were 12 bottles of sunscreen in the cabinets under my kitchen sink. How did they get there? Were they running from a large-scale melanoma scare? There were more bottles than bodies that lived in my house. Our task is not to question why it's in this current state but how we are going to tackle this area.

Start small. Do your clean sweep of the floor and counter areas first. Sweep things into a pile to see what you have to pick up, toss, or send packing to the room where it actually resides. Trash anything rusty or crusty that you haven't used. This includes cracked dishes, rusted pots and pans, and broken utensils. Use the 10-second rule to release items you may feel particularly attached to that are impractical or have no use. The first step is about getting rid of the garbage, like old scrubbing pads, smelly sponges, expired products, and empty cleaning bottles.

The next step is to pick a place to start deep cleaning. I recommend attacking your junk drawer. If you have more than one, work on one drawer at a time, only starting another when you have completely finished the first. Even if this drawer is the only thing you get completed (after your initial clean sweep, of course), still count it as a major accomplishment and celebrate it. Remember, Rome wasn't built in a day.

Are you a coupon-collecting family? Now is the time to get rid of all your old coupons and restaurant takeout menus. Those things will keep coming every week with your junk mail and whenever you order out. Free yourself of the old, and create an organizer for the new by using a file box or stacker from your local office supply store. Go paperless by making use of online coupons. You can get them on your phone and scan them electronically at checkout. You can find online coupons on retailmenot.com or your local supermarket website.

Do you have an array of coupons for things you don't use or expired coupons in your drawer? Send them to military families overseas. Military families can use manufacturer's coupons for up to six months after the expiration date at the commissary. Check out supportourtroops.org/troopons for more information. Be sure to follow the instructions closely. You can clean out and give to families in need at the same time.

To keep the chaos at bay, take 30 minutes once a month to purge your paper and online coupons. Commit to 10 minutes once a week to purge sales flyers. Once you begin to do this consistently, you will find that it will take you less and less time to complete. It is those first steps that are the hardest.

If you choose a shelf in your cupboard or kitchen cabinet, empty the shelf first and wipe it down. A clean, clear shelf will give you a sense of accomplishment. Check for expiration dates on all canned goods and containers. Trash those that are no good. Do you have a stack of lids with no containers to match? If you have younger children, let them play matchmaker with the tops and bottoms. Set a timer and make it a game to see how fast they can do it. Think of the game *Perfection* from the Milton Bradley Company produced in the 1990s. In that game, you had to fit all the different shaped pieces into the board before the timer went off and tossed everything out. Toss out any bottoms that are cracked and any tops that don't have a bottom.

If you are starting by cleaning your refrigerator, pick one shelf at a time. Clear the shelf or area entirely, then wipe it clean of all the sticky-icky stuff that gets spilled, rots, or smells. Throw out anything that looks like a lab experiment. If it's molded and stored in a plastic container, toss the container with the spoils as plastic can hold bacteria even after cleaning. The rule of thumb is, if it's molded, don't hold it. Recycle empty containers that are clean and clear of moldy oldies. If you aren't going to use that butter container right away, trash it. You don't want an entire collection of miscellaneous debris. Label containers with the date the item was refrigerated so you have an automatic visual of when it should be tossed.

Check out build.com or amazon.com for ideas on cabinet and kitchen organizers. Cutlery organizers, tiered wall mounted storage racks, pantry and under-the-sink organizers can be used to contain the products you use every day. Check out your local Dollar Store to save money on some of these items.

Decluttering your kitchen saves you time and money, probably more than any other area of your home. Items in your kitchen are predominantly perishable. Waste is costly, especially in today's economic atmosphere. Once you know exactly what you do and do not have, you won't fall into the trap of buying more than what you need.

Check out these other ideas for clearing and cleaning:

- **Clean as you go.** As you are cooking, wash used utensils, dishes, pots, and pans. Dry them and put them back in their proper place as soon as you are done with them. By the time dinner is ready, half the work of kitchen cleanup is already done.
- **Share the load.** Assign weekly dish days or kitchen cleanup chores for children living in the home with you. Ask a significant other to help. Make after-dinner cleanup family bonding time.
- **Hire help.** If you are a caregiver of an older adult or a child with special needs, hire someone to come in once or twice a week to help you keep this area clean and neat. Is there a teen in the neighborhood you know and trust, a mature woman looking for something to do, or an elderly woman who wants to help out and is good with children? Check with doctors, religious organizations, and community service organizations to find free or low-cost assistance.
- **Have a specific place for things.** This will make it easier for your family to keep the chaos at bay. Use bowls for keys, drawer organizers for odds and ends, and tiered baskets or shelving for other items.
- **There's no such thing as free.** Just because something is free doesn't mean it's beneficial. Before you accept that free item, ask yourself how much space it will take up, if you will really use it, and how it benefits you. Accepting free stuff that ends up in a drawer somewhere costs you time, and time is money and health. Think about how that one little thing can add or subtract from your life.

- **Recycle right away.** If you're considering recycling an item, do it right away. The longer you hold on to it, the less likely you will do what you need to do to repurpose it. Is the process of recycling even worth your time? If not, trash it or donate it.

The kitchen is the heart of the home. It is the place where families gather for nourishment of body and soul. It is the hub, the center for guests, laughter, and love. Work your way around this space by tackling one area at a time. This makes the entire process less overwhelming. Once you complete your decluttering and reorganization, you will not only free the heart of your home, you will free yourself.

IT'S A WASH

Laundry is my personal nemesis. I know I'm not the only one who has been discouraged by overflowing baskets of dirty clothes and piles of used linen. If you have tweens and teens, you've probably also had the experience of the laundry mix. You know, when your child or partner mixes the dirty and clean clothes together so everything is funky. Now you have to wash everything because of all the blended odors. How frustrating and time-consuming is that?

The purpose of a laundry room is to get things clean, so it makes sense to clean the laundry room itself first. Start with a clean sweep of the floor. Get the dust bunnies hopping out of the corners. Clobber the cobwebs. Empty trash bins and lint collectors. If your laundry room is in the basement, focus on the area around the washer and dryer. Get behind your washer and dryer with a grabber or duster to clear up anything that may have fallen back there on laundry day. If your laundry area is only a small closet space or a corner in the kitchen, the same things apply.

After you've cleared the floor areas, declutter shelves and storage spaces. Do you have several bottles of detergent but none are full? Can you combine them into one and throw away the extra containers? Look at your space. Is there room for wall-mounted shelves, a door for hanging an iron, or a collapsible table? What is your vision for this area? Is there a scheduled laundry day or time? Who takes care of this chore? Laundry duty is something everyone can get involved in to some extent. Ideally, what would the in- and outflow of laundry look like for you and your family?

Once you have created a vision for your laundry area, use some of these creative ideas from *Woman's Day* (Dubin, 2022):

- Use a three-piece hamper to separate clothes by color after they've been worn. Teach your children and partner how to use this hamper so you have less work to do on laundry day.
- Add a folding station to your laundry area. This can be a small shelf or a folding table that can be easily stored.
- Use decorative bins and baskets. Woven ones are prettier than plastic and can add some beauty to an otherwise boring chore.
- Use a collapsible drying rack. This can hang on a wall or a door.
- Don't waste wall space. Use it to mount shelves, hanging laundry baskets, or a fold-out table.
- Roll towels to save space in your linen closet and laundry area.
- Hang the ironing board on the prongs of a towel rack.
- Create containers for all the things that come out of the wash, like stray buttons, hair clips, and other miscellaneous items. Use pretty jars that you can buy at the local discount store or recycle jars from fruits and jams for lost buttons and other small items.

- Use magnetic bins on the sides of your washer and dryer for additional storage.
- Use small wall-mounted baskets for stray socks. Make a plan to reunite lost socks by having a lost sock bin. You can mix and match from one laundry day to the next.
- Make this utilitarian space more inviting by adding some decorative touches.

Make sure whatever method of organization you use fits your lifestyle. Modeling your rooms on the way other people do things might not work out so well. Keep yourself and your family in mind when adding, minimizing, and organizing. Create drop zones according to the flow that works for you.

NO PARKING ZONE

Remember all those bags of clothes you gathered to give away? Did you stack them in your garage instead of actually giving them away because there was no time between athletic runs for kids, grocery shopping, and work? Have you just moved boxes from one place to another? Has your garage become a no parking zone? Thou shalt not fool thyself with excuses. If your car is parked at the curb instead of in the garage because there's no room where it belongs, it's time for a change.

You can reclaim your garage if you have a plan. Before you go out and buy a bunch of organizational tools, including storage bins, racks, and other solutions, decide what your garage is going to be used for. Is it currently a storage space, workout space, woodshop, or a combination of things? Figure out what your main purpose is going to be for this area.

Next, prepare for cleaning day. Because you will remove everything from the garage on cleaning day, pick at least two consecutive weekends to tackle this project. If your garage is a major cluster hub, you may want to stretch the process over several days. Before starting, get your cleaning equipment ready, including brooms, dustpans, trash bins, a dumpster if necessary, work gloves, and a face mask. If you want to give your garage a lift, choose a paint color for the floor and walls that will make the area more inviting. Think about how you want to feel rolling into that space, especially on days where you need a few minutes of downtime before dealing with family.

Once you have a clear space, you can envision how much floor space you'll need for parking, lateral space for opening and closing car doors, and head space for things you want to hang from the ceiling. Consider getting as many things up off the floor as possible. Think about those things you would like to access easily, like bicycles, tools, lawn equipment, and snow shovels.

Once you've put the garage project on your calendar and envisioned what you want, begin the work. Follow this list of do's and don'ts to get it all done (Mom Can Fix It, 2021):

• Get help if your garage has been used as a storage space or if you think it's going to be a pretty big job. Enlist assistance from family, friends, and neighbors. Even the dog can pitch in if you have one big and strong enough.

• Empty your garage completely and give it a good cleaning. Paint walls and ceilings according to your preference. Make sure to wear work gloves and a face mask to keep all the dust, dirt, and sharp things from hurting you.

- Begin to set up your storage spaces once your cleaning is done.

    - Avoid buying storage solutions and equipment until you are really sure what you need to store. Purchase necessary items only after you establish a clearly defined plan. This way you won't overspend or crowd the space with more overabundance.

    - Use wall mounts for bicycles, camping equipment, ladders, and large lawn, garden, and workout equipment.

    - Add sturdy overhead racks that can hold equipment you don't use every day but still find necessary to store or keep.

    - Invest in large, clear bins and categorize the things that go in each. For example, gardening tools, sports equipment, and collectibles can all go in different bins. Label them so they will be easy to recognize. Clear bins are easier to identify things on sight and from a distance.

- Stay focused on the garage project. Don't get distracted by the things that can become a project within a project.

    - Concentrate on organizing the garage first. If something in the garage needs repairing but the need is not immediate, complete the repairs afterward.

    - Avoid putting off repairing something that is in immediate need of fixing. You don't want to have to clear the garage again to fix something you could have taken care of during the clearing phase.

- Organize bins as you go using the toss, keep, or donate system. Start by clearing one wall space at a time. Don't add shelving or storage solutions until the garage is completely clean.

- Purchase or build utility shelving. It is a must for garage space. Check out your local Home Depot or Lowe's hardware stores for storage solutions and classes on how to complete do-it-yourself (DIY) projects to enhance your garage space. Home Depot offers free workshops at many of its stores.

- Drive your car in and mark where it clears the space from the garage door once your floors and walls are clean, clear, and painted, and any necessary repairs have been completed. Take some iridescent yellow tape or yellow paint and mark the spot. This way you can ensure that you are always far enough in to keep the garage door from slamming down on your vehicle. Mark in the front as well so you and any other drivers can see the boundaries in front and behind.

- Place storage bins on your shelves and set up your wall racks for other equipment and belongings after you have marked your territory.

Consider renting a dumpster if you have a garage that is overcrowded with things you will have to dispose of. This includes packaging for new pieces of hardware, equipment, and storage solutions. Research available companies in your community or call your city's parks and recreation department to see when they pick up bulk trash. If you opt for a dumpster, place it in an inconspicuous space so you don't have neighbors filling it up with their junk. Set a date, day, and time for delivery and pickup.

When you have completed revitalizing your garage, do a happy dance. I mean it. Turn on your favorite song and rock out! You've done it again. Celebrate your awesomeness!

A FEW TOSS, KEEP, OR DONATE RULES AND SUGGESTIONS

Deciding whether to toss out, keep, or donate an item can be tricky and emotional. You may want to keep some things that, though they have no monetary value or usefulness, still have sentimental value. So how do you decide?

With each item you touch, ask yourself what value, if any, it has to you. Some examples of items families commonly keep are (Hide-Away Storage, 2020)

- winter clothing that will still fit next year
- clothing that still fits, looks good, and is in style
- anything with strong sentimental value
- items very high in monetary value that can be sold if not in perpetual use
- sports equipment you still use
- winter bedding in good condition like comforters, blankets, and linens

"One man's trash is another man's treasure" holds true, but not all the time. What has no more significance for you, may be just the thing another person needs. You can sell your used items online or at a yard sale or donate them to charities like Goodwill, Salvation Army, Purple Heart, and domestic violence housing projects. But all trash isn't treasure. Don't go donating that dusty toothbrush that's been hanging around your bathroom for half a decade, even if it's sealed in packaging. Check shoe soles and heels for holes and wear. Avoid donating that old shirt that a swift wind will turn to dust. Ask yourself if the item you are considering donating is in good working order and if it has any possible value to another person. Think of yourself as the person on the receiving end. Would you want to get what you are giving?

Charity organizations usually have a list of things their clients need. Each organization is different. Call ahead to see what they are in need of or what kind of donations they accept. Just because you don't want it, doesn't necessarily mean someone else does. Some organizations will come pick up the donation, saving you time and gas. Others will require you to drop it off. Incorporate time for that process.

Letting go of our memorabilia is the hardest thing in the world for us humans to do. We have become attached to old papers, pictures, postcards, kids' drawings, our first love letter, and the ballet shoes and prom dress we can no longer wear and don't need. Recognizing that one day, someone else will be burdened with all the things we held onto puts some of it in perspective.

Wendy Lustbader, MSW, affiliate associate professor at the University of Washington School of Social Work offers (Lustbader, 2022):

> You instantly realize that most of your accumulation will one day be dumped into a recycling bin. The things you are saving as reminders of your past are useless to others. Sure, you may value what you keep, but worth is arbitrary, personal, and essentially all in your head.

How much stuff would your children, grandchildren, or significant other have to purge if you no longer existed? Would they be stuck with a mess, or are you right now creating wonderful memories for them to keep in their hearts? Ms. Lustbader calls the work of "clearing out the superfluous" a spiritual practice. As we are able to relinquish our hold on things from our past, things we no longer have any use for, things that generations following us will see no value in, we release ourselves and our loved ones. Purging your memorabilia may be time-consuming and emotional, but letting go of all those old cards from your 18th birthday party will free you to live today.

5

DIGITAL CLUTTER—A WALK THROUGH YOUR COMPUTERS, TABLETS, AND PHONES

Laura's social media life is out of control. Slack notifications from her team at work, Facebook and Instagram notifications from the kids, private messages from friends, and texts from the hubby, clients, Mom, Dad, and relatives are giving her anxiety. She feels pulled in a thousand directions and is constantly distracted and on edge. All the dings, bells, and whistles are driving her crazy!

INFORMATION OVERLOAD

Have you ever jumped out of the shower soaking wet, barely taking the time to wrap a towel around yourself in order to catch that phone call before it stops ringing? Have you ever scrolled your social media while on the toilet? Come on, admit it. Haven't you reached for your cell phone at the most inconvenient times? In our digital world, notifications are a constant distraction drawing us into a labyrinth of unnecessary information.

Digital clutter has the same impact on time management, health, and well-being as physical clutter. At work, you may feel scattered between two computers with multiple open tabs. At home, there are phone calls to make and receive, texts to send, and apps to download, upload, and reload. We carry cell phones from the bedroom to the bathroom and everywhere in between. We are constantly connected and disconnected at the same time, even alone together.

No matter where you are, you are assaulted with information, whether you want it or not. Ads are on public transportation, cars, trucks, the radio, and television, as well as at the doctor's office, your workplace, and your favorite restaurant. Everything has an app to download, a website to check out, and an insta-something or other. Long gone are the days of encyclopedia salesmen. Analytics check out everything you look at and purchase, and then decide what ads will come to you through the internet, social media, and mail. It's exhausting.

The dangers of information overload include fatigue, depression, stress, burnout, and a host of other psychosomatic complaints. Creativity decreases because a brain clogged with miscellaneous ideas can't think of new ones. There just isn't room. The desire to know what is happening at every moment of the day has put us on alert all the time, increasing cortisone to dangerous levels, affecting us as much physically as psychologically.

Think about any time you have ever been assailed by bill collectors, fundraisers, and politicians through text messages, emails, phone calls, and junk mail. It's like being attacked by a swarm of bees looking to you for honey. You don't even make honey! It's too much. Time to power down and screen your information processes.

WE INTERRUPT THIS PROGRAM...

Life is busy. We rely on our technological devices to get things done more quickly and efficiently. Trying to refocus after a venture into the matrix of miscellaneous data and entertainment, we can lose sight of what's really important. Why did you dive into the vortex in the first place? Were you looking for something specific, or were you just bored? Do you believe you are an expert at multitasking and that the monsters can't catch you?

When you do things repeatedly, you train your brain to operate on autopilot. Have you ever driven to work without knowing how you got there? Your brain has been trained to take the same route every day. It even allows for certain kinds of distractions like traffic jams and sudden stops. You actually switch off from time to time while your brain continues to navigate the route. Something different happens when you attempt to do more than one thing at a time. The brain doesn't get a chance to learn the routine and implant it in your memory when it is constantly switching tasks. This can be dangerous, as it may short-circuit your memory, overload mental resources, and impair executive functions like controlling and managing cognitive processes (Cherry, 2019). This won't interfere when you're folding clothes while you're watching the next episode of *The Young and the Ruthless*, but even a few seconds are critical when you're behind the wheel of a 2-ton vehicle going 70 miles per hour. For this reason alone, it is imperative that you clear the information overload you have become so accustomed to.

No matter how much you tell yourself the lie that you are good at multitasking, science has proven that none of us are capable of focusing clearly on more than one or two tasks at a time. Multitasking is an epic myth. Neuroscience research shows us (Napier, 2014):

> The brain doesn't really do tasks simultaneously, as we thought (hoped) it might. In fact, we just switch tasks quickly. Each time we move from hearing music, to writing a text, or talking to someone, there is a stop/start process that goes on in the brain. That start/stop/start process is rough on us. Rather than saving time, it costs time (even

very small microseconds). It's less efficient, we make more mistakes, and over time, it can sap our energy.

Try this test from *Psychology Today,* and you'll quickly see how this works (Napier, 2014):

1. Draw two horizontal lines on a blank sheet of paper.

2. Have someone time you as you complete the following tasks:

a. On the first line, write I am a great multitasker.
b. After you have completed the first line, write the numbers 1 to 20 in sequential order on the second line.
c. Record your time when both lines are completely done.

3. After you have fully completed step two, draw two more horizontal lines. Start your timer and complete the following tasks:

a. On the first line, write the letter "I." On the second line, write the number "1."
b. Go back to the first line and write the letter "a."
c. Go back to the second line and write the number "2."
d. Go back to the first line and write the letter "m."
e. Go back to the second line and write the number "3."
f. Keep going back and forth between lines until you have written the same sentence and numbers that you did in step two.
g. Record your time when both lines are completely done.

You will see a significant difference in the time it takes you to multitask this simple sentence and number sequence. This is your brain when it has to switch tasks. The more your brain has to refocus, the more energy you're using. No wonder you feel so exhausted after a long day at work, especially if your work involves computers, writing or researching information, dealing with numbers, or anything that requires a lot of brain power. The longer you work, the less effective you become. If you don't want your mind to go offline, you will have to interrupt your program and power down for a few minutes to reboot. You will have to download your digital clutter, trash, and recycle. There are even systems on all of your devices specifically for that purpose. When you fail to use these features, your devices short-circuit. You'll know when they've reached their limit when batteries die, your computer shuts down, and your tablet goes haywire. That's your technological brain on overload.

TIPS TO MANAGE DIGITAL CLUTTER

Besides being distracting and annoying, digital clutter can be a brain drain. The fact that today we have extensive access to information we never had before is beneficial, but it comes with a price. Sensory overload decreases mental focus. Bombarded with too much information, the brain goes offline. "The overwhelming amount of information blurs the line between valuable information and distraction and makes it harder for [you] to keep track of and filter information" (Modijefsky, 2021). Here are a few tips to help clear that digital clutter that keeps you so distracted:

• Turn off your notifications. That sounds simple because it is. Do you really have to know when someone posts something to Facebook, Twitter, Instagram, or some other social media outlet? How does anyone's post contribute to your well-being for the day? Are you a publicist, blogger, or in another profession that requires you to keep tabs on these things? If not, turn them off.

- Follow these digital cleanup basics:

  - Unsubscribe from digital newsletters, subscriptions, and other junk mail you aren't using or reading on a regular basis.
  - Delete any apps you aren't currently using, including games, social media apps, and music apps you don't use.
  - Go through your files and purge them of any unnecessary or duplicate information. Get out your digital trash can and dump all the garbage into your recycling bin.
  - Clear your recycling bin at least once a month.
  - Put any loose files into a folder. Everything should have a home in your digital file cabinet. Mark the files with relevant names and dates so you know what and when to archive things you need to keep, like tax information.
  - Clear any archive files that are no longer needed. Cast them into the recycling bin for all eternity.
  - Complete a digital shred for sensitive files just as you would sensitive paperwork.

- Categorize your files with names that are familiar to you and easy to find. You can add subcategories within those general categories if you like. Some categories can include

  - family projects
  - business projects
  - client folders

    *housed by name
    *organized alphabetically or by project

- family history
- family recipes
- school records
- family photos

> *children's photos from childhood to adult
> *grandchildren's photos
> *photos of extended family
> *photos of friends
> *photos of family events

- Keep things as simple as possible. Don't complicate your filing system or make it too detailed to keep up with on a regular basis. Give categories simple headings that you can immediately identify, and avoid adding too many subcategories.

- Group like items together just as you did in your kitchen, bathroom, and bedroom. Keep the essentials at the forefront by making them favorites on your computer or adding icons to easily and quickly access them.

- Create reusable templates that you can share and reuse instead of trying to create something new every time.

- Do the six-month checkup. When you were clearing your closet, you donated things you had not worn in over a year. The same goes for digital clutter. With the exception of taxes, which you keep for at least seven years, and medical records which you can keep indefinitely, toss anything you haven't used for the last six months.

- Separate work files from personal files. You can even go so far as to only keep work files on a work computer, even when you work from home.

- Do a weekly email cleanup:

  - Separate emails into categories.
  - Respond to urgent emails as soon as you receive them.
  - Respond to important emails within 24 hours.
  - Respond to regular emails by the end of the week.
  - Delete junk mail.

- Unsubscribe, delete, and unfollow people you really don't deal with on your social media apps. This way, you will have less unnecessary information clogging your feeds.

- Bookmark items you may use often instead of keeping a bunch of tabs open on your computer. This way, you avoid the stress of seeing so many things at one time and feeling overwhelmed.

- Take 10 minutes at the end of the week to clear your cache and history so you can start fresh the next week.

Gone are the days of the phone hanging on the wall that you had to share with the entire family. Magical phone booths you could duck into, close the door, and ring for help no longer exist in most parts of the world. Now we are tied at the hip to our gadgets, panicking if we should lose sight of them at any moment. More precious to us than our wallets, we hold them tight because they store information about our entire lives. These same digital wonders that were meant for good can cause moments of pure evil. We crave them when we're away from them, panic when we can't find them, and spend hundreds upon hundreds of dollars to acquire the latest updates, best cameras, and most gigabytes (even when we don't understand what gigabytes are).

If your cell phone notifications are sapping your productivity, depleting your energy, and giving you a bad case of the bubble guts every time it pings, sings, or whistles, disengage. Silence your phone between the hours of 10:00 p.m. and 8:00 a.m. Shut it off for a few hours every day as the phone itself needs to power down to operate at maximum capacity. It's true that silence is golden, at least in this case. Allow yourself some peace of mind by getting off the hamster wheel of having to know and do it all. Get yourself healed from the addiction of overstimulation through too much information.

6

MENTAL CLUTTER—SMASHING YOUR LIMITING BELIEFS, INNER CRITIC, AND NEGATIVE INNER CHATTER

Mark Twain said, "Of all the things I've lost, I miss my mind the most." I think every woman I have ever worked with has battled mental clutter, be it what others have said to her, her perception of what's been said to her, or what she thinks about herself. Mental clutter has the same impact as physical clutter. It can show up as low productivity, procrastination, and overwhelm. Many women, especially married women who are also parents, work the second shift after getting home from work. This includes household responsibilities, the kids' and husband's schedules, and their own appointments. There is a constant chatter that goes on in their minds. Am I messing up? Am I doing this right? I shouldn't have said that. What should I have done? Did I get everything done? Is it done right? What appointment did I miss? Why aren't there any matching socks? I'm a bad mom, wife, businesswoman, grandmother, daughter. The list goes on and on. We clog our minds with self-deprecating remarks when we're feeling overwhelmed and stressed. We become our own worst critics. This negative self-talk affects the way we see and do life.

MENTAL CHATTER AND OVERWHELM

Mental health is a very popular topic these days, and it's a good thing too. It used to be taboo to talk about the effects of stress on your mental health. Only *crazy* people went to see therapists. Only *hippies* took up meditation and yoga. Now it's mostly mainstream and not a moment too late.

Mental clutter can be debilitating. The combination of your own mental chatter plus chatter you are receiving on a minute-by-minute basis from other sources can make anyone cuckoo for Cocoa Puffs. Your five senses are the primary gates through which information enters the psyche. What you hear, feel, taste, touch, and see can impact your perception, including

- how you view yourself and others
- how you see the world
- how you receive other information
- how you feel physically
- how productive and resilient you are

Hearing and seeing are two of the main ways we receive and process information. If most of the information you are allowing into your space is negative, then you will churn out negative. If it's positive, it's more likely you too will be positive. Input will always equal output. In the last chapter, we discussed the effects of overwhelming digital clutter, that invisible burden we carry when our devices are shouting at us to get work done or watch the next thing. Now that you've cleared some digital space, it's time to clear your mind.

Meditation and mindfulness are well-known for their mental benefits. When done regularly, these activities lower stress, increase productivity, increase a sense of joy and well-being, and free up headspace. As a matter of fact, there is actually an app called Headspace that is especially effective for those who have a hard time shutting down their mind for long periods of time. With Headspace, you can practice meditation and mindfulness for as little as 60 seconds at a time, increasing as needed. It's like a capsule for the brain with a boat load of benefits and no awful side effects.

Mental clearing is done the same way you do every other type of decluttering we discussed. There are only a few differences. You will need a journal instead of a trash can; though you may use a trash receptacle too if you want to burn pages in your journal. (Yes, that is acceptable behavior.) Journaling will also help you organize your thoughts, set some goals, and define your boundaries.

Instead of a tote for giveaways, you can donate your thoughts by using those ideas you've been contemplating. Volunteer to help others. Using your talents and skills to help those who may need them is beneficial to your mental health because when you are helping others, you are not concentrating on your own problems. Use volunteer time wisely. Work with a cause you strongly believe in. Decide beforehand how much of a commitment you can afford to make. Remember, you only get 24 hours in a day. Avoid obligating yourself to the extent that your volunteer work becomes a burden to you or your family.

You're going to toss ideas, information, and emotions out of your mind by journaling. You'll donate by volunteering. You will keep yourself centered through meditation and mindfulness.

You can overcome at least some of the stress of overwhelm by dumping information your mind is exposed to on a regular basis. Keep only what you need. Does that email or text message apply to you? If not, dump it. Don't even bother reading it. Consider it junk mail and trash it. Is it necessary for you to have news at your fingertips every hour of every day? Are you a reporter? Are you involved in some international espionage? If you want to catch up on world news, read one newspaper or view one news program. It is not necessary to have the news on repeat, hammering negative information into your psyche multiple times a day. A good way to clear mental clutter is to only take in what is useful to you at the moment. You can only live one day at a time. Address tomorrow's cares and concerns when you get to them, understanding that tomorrow doesn't exist. There is only today.

SURVIVOR'S GUILT

Survivor's guilt, or survivor's remorse, is another type of emotional clutter. You feel guilty because you survived what and when others didn't. The guilt weighs you down, immobilizing you so that you can't move forward. You sit in life's garage like a parked car with the motor running. You are capable of movement but are too ashamed to put the car in drive. You can't function at maximum capacity. You experience feelings of unworthiness and sadness. You may have escaped the fire, but your siblings, parent, or child didn't. Why were you saved? Questions abound in your mind. You feel like your survival is unfair.

You can also experience survivor's guilt if someone died trying to save you, or you survived but couldn't save others. Survivor's guilt is often associated with post-traumatic stress disorder (PTSD), though everyone who has PTSD doesn't always have survivor's guilt, and vice versa. If you have experienced a medical trauma, loss of a family member or friend, or loss of others during a natural disaster, you may experience some of the most common physical and psychological symptoms below (Cherry, 2021):

- difficulty sleeping
- appetite changes
- headaches
- nausea or stomachache
- racing heart
- feelings of helplessness
- flashbacks of the traumatic event
- irritability
- lack of motivation
- mood swings and angry outbursts
- obsessive thoughts about the event
- suicidal thoughts

Persons with a history of trauma, depression, low self-esteem, lack of support, and poor coping skills may be more inclined to experience survivor's guilt. If you are a person who tends to internalize blame, you too may experience survivor's guilt when faced with a traumatic situation. You ruminate about how things could have been different if you had done something different.

Methods used to treat persons dealing with survivor's guilt can include cognitive behavioral therapy (CBT), group therapy, support groups, and medication. Other strategies include the following (Cherry, 2021):

- Allowing yourself to grieve. Grief has its own trajectory. It's different for everyone. It is human to acknowledge that people were lost and that tragedy happened.
- Forgiving yourself whether you were at fault or not. All humans make mistakes. It's a part of life.
- Volunteering or doing something positive to serve yourself and others. Be the change you want to see in yourself and in the world at large.

- Shifting your focus to the externals leading up to the event rather than blaming yourself.
- Remembering that feelings of guilt, fear, sadness, anxiety, and grief are normal after experiencing a tragedy.
- Getting help if the overwhelm becomes too much.

THE IMPACT OF MENTAL CLUTTER

We are exposed to copious amounts of information daily. Your brain filters that information and holds onto what it feels you need. It stores anything received repetitively in the hippocampus, our memory bank. These memories can be retrieved at any time, whether we want that file opened or not. It can be difficult to stop this mental chatter from damaging our perception. That's why it is imperative to be conscious of what we are feeding our minds.

Your brain is a highly sensitive instrument that filters information, processes it, files it, and uses it when necessary to protect you. Your brain on junk food has a high intake of violent television (including the news), copious hours of scrolling through the internet or social media, or reading every porn magazine you can find. This brain often judges itself and others, finding everyone guilty. It may be full of conspiracy theories and other unfounded information. It may show up as anger, distrust, verbal attacks, and other negative communication.

A brain gone wild is usually filled with anxious thoughts about a past you cannot change or a future you cannot presently grasp. This brain is filled with false perceptions and False Evidence Appearing Real (F.E.A.R.), which causes you to Forget Everything And Run! This brain burns out quickly because of the copious amounts of energy it takes from all the cells to empower the flight, fight, or freeze response. When you can't sleep no matter how fatigued you are, your brain may be on an overdose of epinephrine, better known as adrenaline.

The word *mindset* has a lot to do with the way your mind is trained to respond to outside stimuli. It has to do with your attitude, how you process information, and what information you allow into your psyche. Do you blow up easily? Does that mean you have an anger management problem, or do you just have too much on your plate? Or do you read or expose yourself to a great deal of negative information? This can affect your mindset. It's simple: What you set your mind on becomes your reality. You can't get pears from an apple tree, no matter how much you want it to be that way. In the same way, a mind cluttered with negative input will make you more reactive than responsive.

If you want to unplug from the clutter that is clogging up your brain and receive the benefits, or fruit, of a mind at ease, you have some work to do. Following are some ways to remove mental clutter:

- Set clear boundaries at home and at work. Don't discuss work problems at the dinner table. Keep the two separate as much as possible. Share good news, but keep bad news at bay any time you are breaking bread. Think of other things you can talk about that are uplifting and positive.
- Keep a journal to vent so you don't dump on people at home or at work. Writing it out helps us to dump and clear. You can always burn and throw out what you've written. Write it out by hand instead of writing on your technical devices so that you can easily destroy it.
- Practice mindfulness to keep a clear mind. Be present when you are at home with your loved ones. Be equally present when you are on the job. Silently count to ten (or even three) so you can respond rather than react.

- Understand that everything doesn't need your attention. Millions of thoughts come and go in our minds all day every day. Acknowledge them and let them pass like a car signaling to get in your lane. Let it go ahead of you and keep it moving. Detach yourself from thoughts of the past or the future. Plan your way but be open to the possibility of change.
- Create a space and place for everything and make sure to place it there. As you clean the clutter in your home and in your office, your brain will also clear. If you make a habit of putting your keys in the same place every day, you help your brain remember without having to think about it.

You can clear the clutter in your mind by finding a mindfulness method that suits you. Whether that is stretching, pilates, meditation, praying, or standing by the ocean, find something that resonates with your soul and brings you peace. Remember that a mind at ease is a balanced mind, and a joyful heart is like medicine.

CLARITY AND KINDNESS

A cluttered mind is one in which there is so much going on upstairs that you lose track of anything going on around you. When you are depressed or sad, you become less energetic and less aware of what is going on around you. You can disconnect from your life. This disconnection can show up in disorganization, uncleanliness, and clutter. One way to relieve mental anguish is to be kind to yourself.

The way we do one thing is often the way we do everything. When your mind is cluttered, it flows out into the atmosphere around you. When your space gets cluttered as a result of an overwhelmed mind, you often feel guilty. This becomes a concentric circle, like the proverbial hamster wheel.

One of the most difficult things about decluttering is the guilt we feel in letting things go. When you have lost a loved one, for example, letting go of any of their clothes, papers, other material goods, or even information on a laptop can feel like you are losing your loved one again. It can be an extremely emotional process. You may need the assistance of others to move forward. We become mentally attached to things that were part of our loved ones' lives.

Clutter that builds up when we are depressed can result in anxiety. Compulsive hoarding can also be the result of mental illness. Hoarding can be caused by loss, grief, anxiety, and depression. A person who hoards may not feel they are doing anything wrong, while their family and friends feel like they are drowning in chaos and disorder. This can also be mentally taxing to those they love.

When you are overwhelmed, you are unclear. It's like living in a fog. You feel like you are all over the place, your mental capacities scattered so thin you may feel as if you are going to shatter into a million pieces. This can come from trying to be everything to everybody. Women, especially those in their midlife, suffer this fate due to socialized behavior we learned in childhood. You may be constantly trying to live up to those expectations ingrained in you from the days when women were the primary caregivers, cooks, cleaners, and bottle washers. Establishing boundaries will help you get clear on what you need and want. Remember that you count too. Your needs count. Your desires count. Your dreams and goals count. You are as important as your loved ones, your family, your boss, your friends, or anyone else you serve and care for.

Renowned author and speaker, Brene Brown, said that being clear in what we want and need is the kindest thing we can do for the people we love and care about and for others as well. When we are not clear about our boundaries, when we expect what we haven't even spoken about, it can be very confusing to those with whom we interact. Not talking about your feelings as they arise can cause a backup in your mind that suddenly explodes on someone at the most inopportune times. Ms. Brown encourages folks to have the hard conversations, to confront troubling issues, and to air out their grievances so they can move forward. In this way, one is able to lay aside the weights of guilt, fear, and compulsion (Brown, 2018).

Being kind to yourself is one type of mind clearing we are all capable of doing. Kindness is a gift we so often give to others but, for some reason, withhold from ourselves. Clarity is a kindness to ourselves. When you are clear about your intentions, priorities, values, mission, or purpose, it is easier for others to relate to you. Clutter causes confusion, whether it is in the mind or in the physical atmosphere. The clearer you are in your mind and actions, the less confusing your motives are to others. Confusion creates an atmosphere of distrust, but clarity has the opposite effect. Confusion causes us to feel disoriented. Clarity helps us feel stable. Clarity is a kindness because it gives us peace and a clear sense of purpose. So be kind to yourself by doing the following:

> **Set boundaries.** What are your non-negotiables? What things are you willing to negotiate? What are your deal breakers? Make those things known to anyone you are in a relationship with, whether it is your job's human resources personnel, your husband, or your children. Set boundaries for your children and consequences for when they cross the line. In doing so, you will teach them how to be clear and transparent too.

Manage time wisely. Be conscious of how you spend your time. Give yourself time every day for your mindfulness method or for quiet time alone to relax. It may be five minutes in the car, an hour at the gym, or a half hour walk around the block. Make time for you between all that you have to do in your day-to-day tasks. When you snatch a few moments to yourself every day, you can learn to respond with clarity rather than react in anger and confusion.

Renew your mind. Read books, talk to a friend, get out in nature, journal, talk to a professional therapist, or go on a retreat. All of these things aid spiritual, emotional, and mental healing.

Use positive affirmations to smash limiting beliefs. What you say when you talk to yourself is more important than you may realize. Your subconscious mind doesn't know truth from fiction. It records everything as truth. Shift your attitude by speaking positively to yourself using "I Am" statements in the present tense. Your mind will work out ways to do what you program it to, so program it with your goals when you wake up and right before you go to bed. Make sure your statements contain only positive terminology. Add enthusiasm, emotion, and action to your words to manifest more quickly. A few examples of positive affirmations are below:

- I am a successful entrepreneur.
- I am a great mother, daughter, and friend.
- I am clear and organized in my intentions and actions.
- I am a money magnet.
- I reach my goals easily and effectively.
- I am grateful for all that I have and am.
- I am more than enough.

- I am destined for greatness.
- I am a great problem solver.
- I am a champion because I am conquering my fears every day.
- I am taking the necessary steps to change my life. I am creating a better future.

We all grow up with beliefs that create the patterns of how we live our lives. Limiting beliefs can keep us stuck. Once we identify what those negative belief patterns are, we can begin to break them. These beliefs have become a habit. Habits are ingrained over time. In order to break these habits, you need to do the following:

- Identify the negative beliefs that are holding you back.
- Write them down.
- Write "true" or "false" next to the belief. For example, your limited belief might be that you can't make enough money, that money always runs out before the month. Write down the reasons why you believe this. Keep asking why until you get to the root cause. You may find that the real reason you don't attract money is because you are repelling it with beliefs that money is evil.
- Write a positive affirmation concerning your negative belief. In algebra, a negative and a positive negate each other. Negate your negative beliefs with positive affirmations and action. A positive affirmation concerning money could be, "I am free of limiting beliefs concerning finances. I am extremely grateful that money comes to me quickly and easily now."
- Do things that are consistent with this new belief. Open a bank account for money to flow into if you don't have one. Take a sheet of paper and write down where all your money is, including pocket change. Pay attention to your

money. Avoid speaking hostility and negativity over what you have.

Your mindset makes it possible to overcome almost anything. When you decrease the mental noise, change your attitude with affirmations, and outsource the overwhelm, you will be able to think more clearly and make positive inroads. Clearing the clutter in your mind enhances your health and well-being exponentially.

7

YOUR WORKPLACE—PHYSICAL, DIGITAL, AND MENTAL DECLUTTERING AND PRODUCTIVITY TIPS

Laura's house is organized now. She has taken steps to improve her mental clarity and increase her productivity. But her stress levels go through the roof when she arrives at work. Standing at her desk before she puts down her purse, she sees the pens scattered across it and the Kit-Kat wrapper on her computer keyboard. She seethes inwardly at the person she shares the desk with, the young lady who has left it a mess. A coworker is talking loudly on her cell phone a few feet away. A noxious odor is emanating from another coworker to her left who is eating what appears to be leftover fish from last night's dinner. Last time Laura checked, there was a policy against employees eating at their desks. That's what the cafeteria is for. Laura scans her chair before sitting down, grabs the hand sanitizer to dispense of the candy wrapper and wipe off her keyboard, and finds herself struggling for the rest of the day to stay focused and on task.

WORK-RELATED

You may be in Laura's position. You open the file cabinets at work to find that your coworker has stuffed files underneath the neatly alphabetized or numeric folders instead of in them where they belong. That should be enough, right? Wrong. Your blood pressure goes up three levels. At lunch time, you go to use the microwave, and it smells like seafood. You're allergic. Great! Guess you'll have to raid the candy machine since frozen lasagna pops do not get top billing on your list of favorite foods to scarf down in 30 minutes or less. Then, you walk into the office just in time to hear your supervisor take credit for the project you worked unpaid overtime on. You were so relieved to finish all those emails last night, only to turn on your computer and see 1,000 more. And why in the name of all that is sacred does another coworker have to share all their business and scream at their significant other on the phone during lunch? You go huddle in your car with your Snickers bar meal for relief. How do you manage to get out from under all the chaos and pressure?

Clutter affects productivity. Physical, digital, mental, and audible distractions can literally disrupt your ability to think clearly. Imagine trying to write a research paper in a room full of screaming kids while they are throwing toys at your head. After a while, the mayhem will drastically disturb your sense of calm, no matter how Zen you think you are. At home, you may have some level of control over the madness, but when you work outside the home, controlling the environment isn't always possible. There are numerous sensory distractions, like a woman in a skirt that is way too short and too tight.

LIBERATING YOUR DESK

"Clutter accumulates when we fail to make decisions about things or don't have a good system in place for storing it" (Perrine, 2020). Clutter causes negative feelings as soon as you walk into your office. Minimizing it will increase your productivity and ease your anxiety.

Follow these four basic steps to start organizing (Perrine, 2020):

- Gather similar items together.

    - Band together pens, pencils, and highlighters.
    - Purge and separate papers including sticky notes, memo pads, and scrap paper.
    - Use mini containers to organize small office supplies including staples, erasers, white-out, and paper clips.
    - Use bins for large office supplies including any office equipment that may have to be returned to another department or storage area.

- Contain the items.

    - Use stackable trays for in and out boxes.
    - Use stackable clear plastic totes for large items that must be returned to somewhere outside of your office.
    - Contain blank files in a labeled stand-up file holder that is easily accessible.

- Create a home for the items.

  - Make use of organizers for pens, markers, paper clips, rubber bands, notepads, and other small supplies inside your desk drawers.
  - Use a three-way caddy on your desk to house pencils, pens, and scissors. Keep the caddy organized, refilling it from your drawer supply when needed.
  - Use smaller organizers within your desk drawer to house paperclips, pushpins, and other small items separately so that when you need to clean your desk, it is easy to identify where all the smaller items go.

- Label the items.

  - Label the spaces for each item once everything has a place and you have put those things in their respective places.
  - Label inboxes and outboxes as such so that anyone dropping off papers at your desk can see where they belong.
  - Inform your coworkers how your new desk setup works, especially if you share the space with someone else.
  - Put larger items in crates or totes near, not under, your desk and label the containers so your associates know where these things go. You may be able to get help dropping them off in storage areas or returning them to where they belong if they are labeled.

Once you've created your designated spaces and operating systems, educate those you work with so they put things in their proper place instead of dropping them in disarray on your desk.

Organizing your desk space will help you liberate your desk from unnecessary clutter. Take time throughout the day to address files that haven't been put away. Make a habit of shredding unnecessary paperwork. Avoid printing what you can download, and shred those downloaded files when you are finished with them.

Miscellaneous small items scattered across your desk and drawers can leave you feeling scatterbrained. But when there is a place to put these items, you are able to be more productive. Sweep your desk a few times a day, conducting a final sweep at the end of the day. If you share a desk, let your desk mate know of the value and importance of this new operating procedure.

How many times have you searched for the right pen, the stapler, or that random office thing you've thrown into a cluttered drawer? Knowing where everything is creates less stress. You don't have to declutter everything at once. Pick a drawer or space a day until you've completed all your files and spaces. Declutter first; then organize. Set things up in a way that motivates and inspires you. Use rubber bands, sandwich bags, and zip ties for gathering like things together until you have a place for them. Labels don't have to be fancy. Keep it simple.

When you can walk into a clean, organized office space at the beginning of the day, you will feel calmer, more at ease, and ready to work. The more organized you are, the easier the flow of work will be. The less clutter you have around you, the more clearly you will think. The more clearly you think, the more productive and creative you will become.

MEMENTOS AND MISCELLANEOUS

Our lives are cluttered with memories at home and on the job. Professional organizer Peter Walsh describes memory clutter as "the stuff you're worried if you let go of, you'll lose the memory"' (Perrine, 2020). We tend to personalize our office space with our personal memorabilia, whether it's the framed photos of family and friends or the sack race trophy we won at the office picnic. This miscellaneous collection of children's artwork, client thank-you notes, and beautiful pens that no longer work can cause more chaos than calm. Yet, this assembly of goods also makes our space unique and personal. So how do we resolve memory clutter?

You can resolve memory clutter in a manner similar to the toss, donate, and keep method you have used throughout for decluttering. This time, instead of deciding what to keep based on what is logical, you will let how you feel be the deciding factor. Follow these steps to get started (Perrine, 2020):

• Remove all memorabilia from your desk including photos and other keepsakes.

• Place these things in a box and label the box so it doesn't get misplaced.

  • Use a box with a cover on it so you are not looking at these items longingly and thumbing through them every day.
  • Buy a covered box at your local discount store or create one from a shoebox or a box you received a package in.

• Put your things out of sight for five to ten days once you have them boxed and labeled.

• Gauge how it feels to work in your space without them. Do you have a lot more room on your desk? Are you feeling more productive? What do you notice that's different—better or worse?

• Add one or two things that feel important to you after five to ten days if you feel you need to have some memorabilia in your workspace. Choose items that give you a sense of comfort or motivate you.

You can rotate your keepsakes for variety if you like. Maybe one month you display a family picture and your Employee of the Month certificate. The next month, you have your family and another motivating item. Take pictures of things in your keepsake box. Add anything career related to your resume, curriculum vitae (CV), or professional portfolio. Keep memorabilia on your desk to a two-item maximum. Choose to motivate, not detract from, your daily goals by displaying those items that represent your values and help you stay focused.

SENSORY DISTRACTIONS

The office is bustling, the atmosphere charged with intensity. Phones are ringing off the hook. Your coworker is yelling at her child on the phone. Traffic in and out of your cubicle seems to be nonstop, and the music playing on the intercom is grating on your last nerve. The drab, eggshell office walls feel like they are closing in on you. The air conditioner only works in the winter so you suffocate all summer long. Your hands are either sweating or covered in fingerless gloves. The various odors emitting from surrounding desks are both tantalizing and nauseating. How do you operate effectively in all this chaos and distraction? For some people, this feels like home. For others, this sensory overload can be extremely disruptive.

We use our five senses to connect with the world around us. Distractions can occur when too many of those senses are operating at once. The sight of a coworker coming toward you with a stack of papers can cause a fight-or-flight reaction in your gut. The scent of strong cologne or perfume can leave you heady, nauseous, or both. The constant whirring of a machine or loud conversations can be annoying. The heat that makes you sweat, the cold that makes you shiver, and the taste that morning coffee leaves on your tongue can contribute to brain fatigue. "Sensory overload happens when you're getting more input from your five senses than your brain can sort through and process" (Watson, 2018).

Your brain is your body's computer system. It uses the five senses—sight, taste, touch, smell, and hearing—to decode and process information. When there are too many windows open, its function slows down. Too much sensory information at one time can cause it to overheat in a way. You know you need to take a break from sensory overload when you (Watson, 2018)

- have difficulty focusing.
- are extremely irritable and restless.
- are in extreme discomfort.
- are feeling overexcited or wound up.
- feel stressful, afraid, and anxious about your surroundings.
- experience higher levels than usual of sensitivity to textures, fabrics, clothing tags, or other things that may rub against skin.

It is important to recognize and address your sensory triggers. Unchecked, sensory overload can produce chronic fatigue syndrome and generalized anxiety disorder, among other disturbances in your physical body and mental state. Ask yourself what bothers you. Is it flashing lights? Do the sounds of alarms and bells throw you off, or is it loud conversations? Do certain smells or odors make you feel light-headed? Do squishy things freak you out?

You can reduce sensory input in the office by using privacy screens and protective screens that support and protect your vision and the information you are working on. If you feel the need for quiet you can't find in your workspace, find an empty room or a quiet space where you can work outside of your designated area to get that important project completed. Don't limit yourself to the space you were assigned.

If you have an office, close the door to shut out the noise. For an extra quiet workspace, put on some noise-canceling headphones. Be careful with these in the workplace, however. You need to have at least one ear open. Other ways to reduce sensory overload are below (Watson, 2018):

- Identify safe spaces and times for you to work where you will be less triggered. Is it quieter first thing in the morning when everyone is coming in? Do your priority work at that time.
- Write down a plan if you know you are going to be entering a highly stimulating environment, like a big meeting. Share it with someone you trust who will also be at the meeting and able to assist you.
- Use your plan to stay focused on the task at hand.

In midlife especially, you can also be challenged by chronic pain. Chronic pain can be an unnerving sensory distraction. Disorders like fibromyalgia, muscular sclerosis, migraines, and menopause come with their own set of sensory disruptions and flares. It can be extremely challenging to get organized when you are in pain or feeling fatigued from a medical condition. If this is your personal challenge, here are some tips to guide you:

- Be guided by whether you are having a pain-free day or a painful one.

    - Understand pain depletes your energy.
    - Keep in mind that the better the energy, the larger the project you can work on.
    - Choose a small project you can complete while seated if you are having a tough day.
    - Take breaks every 30 minutes whether you are having a pleasant or rough day. This helps you avoid fatigue.

- Allow yourself recovery days.

    - Give yourself recovery time. When you are building muscle, you break the muscle down by using weights. By the same token, you must give the muscle a day of rest to build itself back up again. This process strengthens the muscle. The same occurs with our energy levels.
    - Rest to replenish energy.
    - Make a decluttering plan and factor plenty of recovery days into it if you want to have your space cleared and welcoming for holiday guests or the office audit.
    - Be cognizant of your energy level at all times. If you are feeling wiped out, that is your body's way of telling you it's had enough. Listen and respond accordingly.

- Ditch the perfectionism.

  - Let others help. Sometimes physical and emotional pain can keep us from doing things perfectly. It's okay to rely on others for help, even if things aren't going to be done exactly how you prefer.
  - Choose to be grateful for the support rather than feeling frustrated.
  - Apply the same attitude of gratitude at home. Chances are, while you are coping with your latest pain flare, your home is also gradually becoming messier while your family takes over duties. Communicate your appreciation for any assistance they provide.
  - Prioritize your health. Ultimately, decluttering and maintenance of that decluttered space have fabulous benefits; however, your health ranks higher than your decluttering goals.

Choose to be kind to yourself and tackle your decluttering projects in such a way that supports your health and wellness along with your other endeavors. Release the guilt when you are feeling fatigued. Follow your doctor's orders in regard to your health. Listen to the clear signals your body gives when it is time to rest, whether for a moment or a few days. Choose to lay aside your cape. You don't have to be a superwoman. She doesn't exist in real life.

8

RELEASING THE PAST

The most challenging area of decluttering we need to face at midlife is sentimental decluttering. Midlife is an emotional roller-coaster ride, with loss and grief among the highlights of self-discovery, reinvention, and family milestones. Your children are getting married and having babies. You struggle to let go of their baby booties and hand-drawn kindergarten pictures. You inherit your mother's china collection or your great aunt's ugly dining suite, and it feels wrong to get rid of these things. That guilt may weigh on you so you refuse to give things away that you have no use for. The present determines your future. In order to move forward, you must release the past, especially if items from the past serve no purpose in the present.

EMOTIONAL DISTRACTION

You are born, your parents nurture and protect you, you grow up, and you move away. One day, you have children and repeat the cycle or help others progress through their cycles. You witness your parents aging. Your loved ones pass away. Your friends move away. You change jobs, start a business, move back in with mom and dad or have them move in with you. Midlife with all its ups and downs is a continual event. So much is going on, and we want to hold on to the precious moments we've shared with people we love and care about. We can't let go of the huge tub of photos that we never got around to putting in photo albums, the thousands of pictures and videos on our digital devices, and those memories we fear will fade from our minds. We are emotionally distracted by our pasts.

MEMORY KEEPERS AND THE GUILTY CONSCIENCE

In ancient societies, the history of tribes and clans was passed down through stories by griots or elders. In modern society, women tend to be the family's memory keepers, the historians handing down the culture, mores, and societal norms. Hand-in-hand with this responsibility is the guilt, the feeling of being incredibly disloyal, when contemplating discarding historical items. Because of this sometimes unspoken pledge of allegiance, we keep our great-grandmother's broach, a lock of hair, and cards from family and friends. As the memory keepers and recorders of history, women in midlife can easily get bogged down with traditions, emotional diversions, and feelings of guilt.

Guilt is mental clutter that is linked to our grasp on things that hold memories. William Morris said, "Have nothing in your house that you do not know to be useful, or believe to be beautiful" (Chrissy, 2022). Yet we are plagued with guilt feelings about things we don't want, don't need, and don't like. Maybe you don't want to waste anything. You believe in recycling and preserving the earth so you think that maybe one day you will use those items for something. If so, you don't have to trash them. Sell them on eBay, OfferUp, or any one of many online sales apps. Donate them to

Goodwill, have a yard sale, or host a trunk sale. One man's trash may be another man's treasure.

We also attach to things we buy on a whim like that bright yellow shirt we thought we would wear on vacation. Even though the color hurts our eyes, we still keep it; its price tag still hangs from the sleeve. We don't want to waste money, so we hold onto it, thinking maybe one day we'll put it on. You've already spent the money, and if the item has been stuffed in the back of your closet for more than a month, there's usually no way you're going to get a refund at the full price, if at all. The only way to move on from the guilt of this purchase is to get rid of it. Sell it at a consignment shop or an online store like Poshmark. Maybe you can gift it to a friend who loves loud colors. The sooner you move it out of your home, the freer you will be.

Did someone give you a gift you don't really like? What would you do if your three-year-old brought you a gift of crumpled, dried leaves? How would you receive it? What would you say to the little one who gives from their heart. Of course, you would thank them and take the dusty mass from their extended little hands, but what would you do with it afterward? Would you throw it away in front of them? Would you tell them that crushed dead brown leaves are not a real gift? Would you scold them for bringing garbage into your house? If you're a loving parent, you would accept the gift and wait long enough for your child to forget about it before tossing it. You don't want to hurt your child's feelings.

You can apply this same tactic to anyone who gives you a gift you don't need or can't use. Be honest with the person if you can. Many people will give you a present with a gift receipt in case you don't like it or the item doesn't fit. A gift receipt is the considerate way of allowing people to return the item and get what better suits them. You can also create a regifting box to hold gifts to give to someone else. Maybe you need a last-minute gift for someone at work. Maybe the gift fits in more with your best friend's style or the couple next door. Label the gift with the name of the person who gave it to you, so you don't regift it to them.

A picture is worth 1,000 words and a good way to keep memories of 1,000 things. You don't have to have the actual object in hand to hold onto the memories associated with it. Group things together that have special meaning to you, take a photo, and include the photo in a scrapbook. Scrapbooking allows you to store things creatively in a way that is engaging and fun. Small items like a bookmark, matchbox, or old love letter can fit in your scrapbook. Include them with the stories they represent. That first love letter from your hubby, your first Girl Scout badge, and photos of a favorite aunt or your first car or whatever else is an important part of your story can be included. You can do the project by yourself or as a family project, or you can have someone put your books together professionally. Your scrapbooks can be used as a library of family history that can be passed down or donated.

Everything we own has a memory attached. It is the memory, not the item in particular, that has value. You are not obligated to keep everything that comes through your door. Let go of the guilt that tricks you into keeping things that cause you more anxiety than joy.

SWEDISH DEATH CLEANING

By the time we get to midlife, we have been carrying the emotional burden of stuff for years, even decades. Decluttering relieves you of that burden. Swedish death cleaning is a way to honor the past without feeling smothered, overwhelmed, or just plain sick of being burdened with the daily maintenance of things you don't need.

Your home is your castle, your fortress from the storms outside your door. But when it's filled with material things that do not serve you or spark joy, it may feel more like a prison than a place of peace. You can still honor the past with a few select items you want to keep. Keep in mind that everything you own comes with memories attached. Hoarding all your stuff is an unhealthy way to retain memories. You can learn to let things go by adopting Swedish death cleaning.

Swedish death cleaning is a term used for cleaning in preparation for a person's death. It's a system of decluttering and organizing your home and environment in a thoughtful, loving, creative way to ease the process of transitioning for your loved ones upon your passing. I know that sounds morbid, but you can death clean while you are still alive. Consider any time you have had to clear the items of a loved one who passed. Have you ever had to go through a loved one's things to sort between what was salvageable and what could be tossed, donated, or kept? It can be a very painful process. Think of your children, your spouse, a significant other, a neighbor, or friends who would have to complete this process for you. When you think in these terms, Swedish death cleaning is a gift and an opportunity. If you clear now, you can create space for clarity and real living in the present and in the future.

The main focus of Swedish death cleaning involves three basic components: clothing, items that take up a lot of space and digital files. Closets literally carry a lot of weight. We know from our earlier clearing and organizing that all kinds of things are hidden in our closet space. We covered digital files and how to cleanse them in our last two chapters. Clearing, cleaning, and organizing large items is another important part of helping us feel more at ease in our space. Giving those space-grabbing items away now can cause a great deal less confusion when decisions have to be made about them later.

Here's how Swedish death cleaning breaks down:

- Clothing

    - Start with closets.
    - Toss or donate what no longer fits or is no longer useful. Ask yourself if those gold platform boots you bought in the 70s are really going to come back in style again. And if they are, can you wear them considering you have bad knees and a tricky back? Be brutally honest with yourself.
    - Take your closet down to the bare necessities. What things do you wear on a regular basis? What things haven't you worn in the last year or two? You are changing and evolving. Keep those items that fit who you are now, not who you were ten or even two years ago.

- Items that take up the most space

    - Decide now what to do with large items like furniture and other things that take up space. Are there some things you can do without? Are your living spaces cluttered with odds and ends you have purchased over time? Is there plenty of space to move around in your bedroom, living room, garage, laundry room, and kitchen?
    - Order a dumpster and get rid of broken furniture and other items you can discard immediately.
    - Offer items to loved ones while you are still around if there are pieces you have been thinking of leaving to them in your will. In doing so, there will be no arguments over what to do with it later.
    - Look for whether or not an item is practical to keep, not for whether or not it sparks joy. Are you using the item on a regular basis? If not, who else can use it?

- Consider donating furniture items to a homeless or domestic violence shelter. These organizations usually collect everything from clothing to household goods and even vehicles to help their clients get a fresh start.

- Digital files

  - Keep a record of access codes, passwords, and logins in a notebook or journal you place in a locked file. These are not something your family members will automatically know if they should ever need them. You can also keep this information in a lockbox at a bank or another secure location.
  - Make sure you have a will and separate powers of attorney for your medical care and financial assets. This is necessary for end-of-life decisions that include your banking, finances, and digital information.
  - Declutter your hard drive and desktop on a monthly basis, clear emails daily, and use the methods discussed in Chapter 6 and Chapter 7. The more you get into the habit of doing this, the less information your loved ones will have to wade through to find what they need.
  - Convert snail mail to digital mail or destroy it. Make a daily practice of shredding what you don't need. Again, be brutally honest with yourself. If you don't need the information, toss it.
  - Clear caches, including passwords and credit card numbers, on a weekly basis. Your digital fingerprint follows you from what you like to eat to how you like to spend your time and money. Prevent scammers from using your information to harm you.

Swedish death cleaning encourages you to take a serious look at the things that have deep personal meaning to you. You don't have to wait until late in the game to do it. As a matter of fact, the earlier you begin to use this minimalist method, the more likely you will be to live a life surrounded by things with deep meaning instead of random objects and meaningless purchases.

LETTING GO

A wedding is one of the most memorable times in a person's life, especially for the bride. Many young girls dream of their wedding day. The beautiful gown, the first dance with their new spouse, the towering cake, expensive gifts, and the honeymoon can all bring a sparkle to a young woman's eyes. We can become extremely attached to the special mementos from this one occasion in our lives. It took me 33 years to let go of my wedding gifts. How many of your wedding gifts are still wrapped in plastic and stored in various corners of your kitchen, bedroom, and linen closet? Giving these items away and discarding them seems almost profane. It isn't fair to assume that your children will want all your hand-me-downs either. Saying "no" or "I don't want that" can make them feel guilty. The last thing you want to do is hand down that legacy. Instead of assuming my daughter would want my long-held wedding paraphernalia, I simply asked her what, if anything, she would like to keep. I did not want to burden her with what might be precious to me but have no meaning for her at all.

Baby shower gifts, the macaroni picture frames our children made in school, souvenirs we received as gifts or acquired ourselves on vacation, and antique family heirlooms are all great to have until they aren't. If you're really in love with the object and can find a current use for it, that's great, but holding onto it because it belonged to or was gifted to you by someone you love will make it a burden not only to you but also to those who come after you.

You know you are emotionally attached to something when you

can't let go of it, even when those things are broken or useless. This is a definite issue in the lives of those diagnosed with obsessive-compulsive hoarding disorder. The key to letting go is to first let go of the guilt you associate with getting rid of the object. This calls for strict objectivity. You will have to look outside of yourself. Consider the object through the lens of logic rather than emotion. Does it serve a purpose presently? Why are you so attached? Can it be digitally stored? Is there someone you can pass it on to who may have a better use for it? Is there someone in the family who might treasure the gift more than you?

How about donating that family heirloom to your local historical society or history museum? Historical societies are always looking for pieces to connect people and places through time. Your grandma's linens may pair with a display of dolls or tableware from the era. Old books, toys, and even some clothing would find a perfect home in an historical society. Donating here would allow for a pleasant detachment. You can visit your grandma's doilies any time and share their history with others in your local area and maybe around the world as many of these historical finds travel.

9

MAINTENANCE SYSTEMS AND TIPS

So you've decluttered your home, your devices, your workplace, and your mind. Now comes the fun part. Go ahead and order all those cute storage containers and organizational tools you've had on your shopping list since the day you started dreaming about this decluttering project. Go ahead and organize to your heart's content! Had you done this at the very start, you would be organizing and rearranging your clutter, moving it from one place to another. But now that you've removed what you don't want or need, you can set up simple maintenance systems to keep your wonderful work intact.

UNDERSTANDING YOURSELF

As we discussed in the beginning of this book, it is imperative that you know who you are and what you need. You can only be true to yourself if you know what makes you happy, what makes you feel at peace, and what you desire most. Boundaries are like demarcation lines. They tell you how far you and others can go. Without some rules governing your space, your time, and your belongings, your physical, emotional, digital, and mind clutter can easily get out of hand.

I am an introvert by nature. Introverts tend to be highly sensitive overthinkers. They can have a great deal of mind clutter. To avoid mental burnout, they need to focus on one task at a time to its completion. This frees their minds from processing unnecessary information and helps them focus and gain clarity.

If you are an extrovert, the way you clean and organize may be a little different. Extroverts are used to acting externally with the world. Their clutter will more than likely be in their environment. They thrive in the office's talkative, chaotic atmosphere. They are the life of the party. If you are an extrovert, you may need to have white noise to calm down. A dimmer can effectively bring down the rambunctiousness of an always "on" personality. Extroverts are great at quick changes but are often bored with anything that takes a bit of time, so cleanup for you might be easier if done quickly and with some type of music or other background noise.

If you fall into the introvert-extrovert category, you are a little of both. You are equally at ease in social settings and in silent alone time. For you, a combination of techniques depending on how you feel at any given time is best.

Learning that I was an introvert helped me understand my own needs when it came to decluttering, organizing, and setting personal boundaries. It's much easier to properly define and navigate your nonnegotiables when you can answer the question of who you are and what you want.

Just like the maps you see in a shopping mall that say, "You are here," determine where you are in your life right now. Who are you? What do you want? What sparks joy for you? What are your hot buttons? What things drive you up a wall in relationships, at work, and at home? What are your pet peeves? What things make you laugh out loud and squeal with glee?

See yourself as you are now and imagine yourself as the person you want to be. Do you want to have more confidence, travel more, have more quiet time, or paint the town red? What kind of atmosphere do you need to flourish? What makes you feel at peace? Once you figure this out and understand your personality type, you can set realistic boundaries and goals.

DRAWING THE LINE

When I was in my early thirties, I tried to be all things to everybody. Anybody who has ever experienced superwoman syndrome knows this is a recipe for disaster. The myth of the superwoman causes women to believe they can do it all: cook, clean, and take care of a family, spouse, parents, and themselves without any help. Somehow, we've been convinced we are magical, like the 1970s character Samantha in *Bewitched* or Major Nelson's spritely friend in *I Dream of Jeannie*. If you weren't around in that era, just know these female leads had magical powers that enabled them to clean up, cook a five-course meal, and dress divinely with a twinkle of the nose and a nod of the head. Of course, that's not so in real life. If it were, a lot of women would sign up for that kind of power in a heartbeat.

I burned out from overwhelm in my thirties, long after Jeannie and her magic had gone off the air. My superwoman cape got singed in the heat of a daily life that included more tasks than I could easily handle. You can get so used to people-pleasing and taking care of others that your own needs get lost in the sauce. Then one day, you find yourself frustrated, fatigued, and feeling alone because you haven't set boundaries.

Boundaries are like guard rails that help you maintain your sanity. They are road signs that tell others how far to go and where to stop. They are your lines drawn in the sand, your road maps, and the tools you need to teach others how you want to be treated. When you have no boundaries, you run the risk of being constantly taken advantage of. You have to draw the line somewhere in your relationships, your patterns of behavior, and even the way you work at getting clear in your physical, mental, and emotional space.

If you are an introvert, saying "no" without offering any definitions, reasons, or excuses is one way to set clear boundary lines. This does not come easily to a person who likes to keep the peace and make everyone happy. Having advance escape plans, articulating needs in a clear, concise manner, and not allowing things and people to suck the life out of you are essential tools for an introvert. Energy drainers include perfectionism, overthinking, and overscheduling. Make sure to schedule power down time for yourself in ink. Make this time nonnegotiable. Speak up at work. You don't have to be rude, but do be firm. Train yourself to say "no" and mean it. Let your "yes" be stated out of your desire to do something, rather than guilt, whether the request comes from family, friends, or others in your circle.

If you are an extrovert, you are used to being at the center of things. You don't mind and even enjoy the attention. All eyes on you is a fact of life, but that same focus can cause a different kind of stress. You can find yourself leaning heavily into perfectionism and egotism. As an extrovert, you are engaging, charismatic, and talkative, but you might overstep others' boundaries. Like the song "The Gambler," popularized by country music singer Kenny Rogers, as an extrovert, you have to "know when to hold 'em, know when to fold 'em, know when to walk away, and know when to run." Everything is not your business. Learn to listen actively instead of listening with an answer already in mind. Even if you know you have the correct answer, it doesn't necessarily mean it's time for you to speak on it. Read the room and censor yourself accordingly.

When it comes to decluttering and organizing, compromise is key. Being able to bend and blend is a tremendous part of any relationship. Never compromise your core values and beliefs at the expense of who you are as an individual. Going along to get along is too steep a price to pay for your integrity. Do listen to one another, find common ground, and work together from there. Two heads really are better than one when they're both focused on moving in the same direction.

MORE ORGANIZATION TIPS

Don't stop at decluttering your own spaces. Teach your entire family these decluttering skills. Kids going off to college? Teach them how to minimize and store items in closet-like spaces. Grandchildren coming over to play? Teach them about designated play areas and how to clean up when playtime is over. Living with a partner who's not used to doing housework? Establish open communication to get help and ease some of the workload.

Following are some reminders and additional ideas to help you release mental clutter and overwhelm:

- Get up from your desk. Walk around. Get some water. Take deep breaths and focus on something positive for a few minutes before you return to your seat. Don't sit at your desk working on your computer for hours at a time. This causes brain drain.
- Make a decision. Start with something small. You can open three pieces of mail and file, answer, or trash what you read right away. No moving papers around for another day. If you practice this every day, you will soon develop a habit of answering mail (including emails) the same way on a regular basis. Before you know it, the piles will be smaller and more manageable.
- Whip out that journal, recite some positive affirmations, listen to a motivational speech by Goalcast or a TED Talk

if you are feeling worried, anxious, and overwhelmed. Get the negative out of your head and onto a page. This way, you can figure out the root cause of what's really bothering you, address it, find solutions, and move on. Dumping it onto the written page helps the fog to clear.
- Take a walk. Get out into nature. Observe a tree, listen to a bird, watch squirrels chase one another. When we connect with nature, we connect with ourselves.
- Be a kid again. Take a walk in the park, swing on the swings, slide down the slides, or play tag with your friends. Find wonder in the world. It's truly a marvelous place.
- Make time for fun. It doesn't have to be planned. Dance, jump around, or watch a live comedy sketch. Laugh. Smile more. Turning that frown upside down has some serious health benefits, including strengthening your immune system and helping you to be a happier, more positive, and more balanced person.
- Talk to someone if you are feeling so overwhelmed that you feel out of control. Grab the listening ear of a nonjudgmental friend or seek professional help. Either way, make sure it's someone you trust with your secrets.
- Make frequent use of hug therapy. Give yourself a hug or get one from someone else. A hug helps you feel mentally supported, happy, and protected. Seven hugs a day keep the overwhelm away.

To reduce sensory input on the home front and in the world at large, follow these guidelines (Watson, 2018):

- Ask for what you need. Ask noisemakers to dial it down. Be polite but don't be afraid to be firm when necessary. As the old saying goes, "You can catch more flies with

honey than with vinegar." Be respectful and don't let your temper get the best of you.
- Go to bed at a reasonable hour. Your brain needs the rest. Avoid television and mobile devices for at least two hours before bed as the sensory stimulation can keep your brain awake even when you feel tired.
- Drink adequate amounts of water. Divide your weight by two. This is the amount of water you should drink in ounces daily. The hydration helps your brain maintain peak performance. Avoid substituting plain water with soft drinks, juices, energy drinks, and other fluids. Clear, clean water is best for your muscles, bones, and energy flow.
- Take serious conversations that might involve confrontation to a quiet corner or, better yet, a private area. The fewer distractions the better. Focus on the issue at hand without bringing up superfluous points. Try to resolve the situation in an equitable manner. Sometimes you may have to agree to disagree.
- Eat a healthy meal before you go food shopping. Special offers and taste tests at your local grocer can be very distracting. On an empty stomach, we make frivolous purchases that have little to no nutritional value. Take a list to the grocery store so you are not distracted by sights and sounds. Focus only on the list. Get what you need and go.
- Try noise-canceling headphones to drown out noise if you are working or trying to relax in a public place.
- Do your shopping during the day between Tuesday and Thursday if you can. This way you can avoid long lines and weekend crowds.
- Leave events early so you are not caught up in the mayhem that follows a concert or night out.

Clutter is usually caused by habits we've acquired over time, but habits are subject to change. Clearing a shoe bin by the door before the night's out is a habit everyone in the family can learn. A bicycle rack in the driveway can be a great drop-off spot for kids' wheels. Your honey can learn to drop his dirty laundry in a hamper near the bathroom or someplace close to where they disrobe.

Paper clutter, under-the-desk clutter, and general disorganization are workplace habits that are also subject to change. To establish organizational wellness, try the following techniques (Perrine, 2020):

- Complete a supply sweep several times a day and scoop up those paper clips, binder clips, and pens and put them in their proper places.
- Make sure your desk is clean and clear at the end of the day so you can come in fresh the next day.
- Don't print it if you can download it.
- Shred unnecessary paperwork as soon as you are done with it. Most offices have a shred bin. Your computer may also have shred software on it. Use it.
- Recycle paper by cutting it into small squares and using it in lieu of post-it notes. When you're finished with the notes, be sure to throw them away.
- Write in pencil so you can recycle folders when necessary. The simpler the label, the easier it is to reuse. Labels don't have to be fancy.
- Assess what is hiding under your desk. Decide whether you need to toss it, recycle it, or store it somewhere.
- Create and label drop-off bins near your desk. Use stackable clear bins when possible so you can see what is inside them at a glance.
- Empty bins at the end of the day or the end of the week. Make this an ongoing habit.

Today in our highly digitized society, thoughts are written in sound bites and sent all over the world before we can voice them out loud. We spend thousands of hours alone together rather than really communicating with one another. Below are some tips to help you release some of the anxiety associated with perfectionism and misinformation in the digital age:

- Be cognizant of the fact that life on social media is not real life. Real life doesn't have filters, reels, and instant stories. Don't compare yourself to the images you see online. There are no perfect homes where perfect people live perfect lives. The reality is that we all have junk in our digital closet and elsewhere.
- Be an advocate for social media safety when it comes to your children, grandchildren, family members, and those in your community. Limit screen time and monitor social media access.
- Safeguard your digital devices from scammers, hackers, and others who would use your digital footprint to cause you harm. Change passwords on a regular basis. Encrypt all outgoing information. Don't open suspicious emails. Ask questions. Check sources. Clear caches and lock passwords.

In the previous chapters, you discovered how clutter can become the nemesis of your best life. You learned about the power of visualization and what it means to be a minimalist. You spent copious hours walking through your living room, bathroom, kitchen, bedroom, garage, and laundry room sorting, tossing, and donating. You worked through your mental clutter and brain drain and learned how to release your past. Now, you can begin to really create the life you want.

10

CREATING THE LIFE YOU WANT

You feel amazing and so much lighter after creating space in your environment, on your devices, in your schedule, and in your mind. Now is the time to ask yourself an important question: What do you want to do with your life going forward? Is there travel in your future? Where would you like to go, with whom, and when? What sights do you hope to see? Do you want to go back to college, or have you never attended and want to pursue it now? What's the next adventure for you?

WHERE TO NEXT—YOUR PERSONAL LIFE AUDIT

In the beginning, you charted your course through visualization. Now is the time to conduct a personal life audit to determine where you are versus where you began and to decide where you want to be going forward.

Conducting a life audit is a great way to get a snapshot of what you've accomplished thus far. It's a time to acknowledge and celebrate the goals you've achieved through this process. Have you developed better communication skills with family and friends? Are you listening more to understand as opposed to just waiting for your turn to speak? Are you and your team communicating on the same wavelength? Is your vision toward minimalism or organization? Are you all on the same page? If decluttering has been a solo mission for you, where are you in the process? Have you asked for help when you needed it? How are you feeling?

These questions and those that follow are designed to help you create or re-create the road map from here (where you are now) to there (where you're going next). Write down the answers in your journal. In a few months, take a look at what you've written. Once again, see how far you've come and what work is left to do. Resist the urge to judge yourself. You don't have to be concerned with dotting every *i* and crossing every *t*. Done is better than perfect, especially when there are deadlines to meet and other work to be completed. As long as you're living, you will always be a work in progress, so forgive yourself when you mess up, regress, or get tripped up.

Next Questions

- What did you dream of doing when you were a kid? Are you doing it now? If not, what's holding you back?
- What kind of lifestyle would you live beyond material things if money wasn't a concern? Would you be trekking through the Everglades, sitting on the grand porch of your spacious home sipping a morning mimosa and watching the grass grow, or would you be doing something else?
- Attitude is a choice. What's yours? Do you wake up grouchy, screaming at the alarm clock, or are you pleasantly making pancakes for the children? You may

not be able to change your circumstances, but magic happens when you change your attitude.
- What's the silver lining in your present cloud? Are you a victim of your circumstances, or are you discovering new opportunities despite your circumstances?
- A smile automatically generates enthusiasm. When was the last time you used one? What gives you a good belly laugh?
- What do you hope for? What makes your eyes light up? What encourages, sustains, and motivates you?
- Who are your five closest friends? What do they do? What are their goals, hopes, and dreams? Do they align with yours?
- Are you and your significant other compatible? Do you feel more connected? Are you on the same path?
- Are you solution- or problem-oriented? Do you focus on the negative or the positive?
- What do you say when you talk to yourself? Are you as loving, compassionate, and caring to yourself as you are to others, or do you talk down on yourself?
- How do you solve problems or resolve issues?
- Do you wallow in self-pity, or are you able to face things head-on and let them go?
- What's your gratitude quotient? How thankful are you? List at least three things you are grateful for today.
- What sparks joy for you?
- What have you learned about yourself on this journey?

Visualization enables you to keep hope alive. Self-evaluation makes it easier to establish fresh insight. It gives purpose and meaning to your goals. Read through the answers to your questions. What do your results reveal? Are you speaking negatively about yourself? Know that when you talk down on yourself, you automatically negate your opportunity for advancement in life and relationships. What you say to and think about yourself matters. Speak to yourself with compassion and care.

What kind of company do you keep? Are your friends forward-thinking, open-minded, positive people? When we were kids, our parents told us to be careful who we hung around. They said things like, "Bad company corrupts good manners," and they told us this or that person was a bad influence. We are either inspiring one another or influencing each other on some level. You will become like the people you associate with the most. If those people are negative, you will find yourself becoming like-minded. Remember your parents' advice and watch the company you keep. Find a group of people, or even just one person, who motivates and inspires you to be and do better. Find a mentor who aligns with your goals and dreams. Whether you get together in person or meet through a Zoom session, connect with someone who is where you want to be.

Your attitude is just as important as, if not more important than, the company you keep. Refuse to whine, groan, and complain. Work on becoming more solution- instead of problem-oriented. To achieve long-term goals, focus on your small daily habits. Examine them to determine what works and what needs improvement. When in doubt, create a pros and cons list to use for decision-making. My book, *21 Hacks to Rock Your Midlife—Release the Past, Dare to Dream, and Create Your Legacy*, features more specifics and action steps to decluttering and reaching your midlife goals.

Great men and women have accomplished spectacular things by keeping their eyes on the prize, even when victory was not imminent. At one time, believing in myself was a challenge for me. As an artist, my knees buckled at the thought of performing in front of audiences. I was torn many times between making a great escape and staying to present my gifts to the world. I learned that it's okay to be afraid and unsure. Courage is certainly not the absence of fear. Change requires bravery. Strong men can overpower others, but the mighty overcome themselves. For this reason, there is tremendous value in taking the time to self-audit. Self-evaluation empowers you to create your personal road map for your next steps. To keep hope alive, visualize.

BUILDING BLOCKS—AUDITING YOUR ATTITUDE, TIME, AND ATTENTION

What was the last thing that made you laugh until you cried? Laughter is healing. It massages your organs and lengthens your days. The more you laugh and smile, the more positive you are. It takes more muscles to frown than it does to smile. Since smiling is a lot less work and has many more health benefits, it makes sense to do more of it.

Attitude is everything. You can't prevent bad things from happening. It's the yin and yang of life. But you can choose your attitude in any given situation. Being positive causes your brain to think of new ways to approach problems. It's much easier to find solutions when you are open to receiving them than it is when you are closed-minded. The easiest way to develop a positive mindset is to be grateful. Thank someone who opens the door for you, cooks you a meal, or hands you a receipt. It's not rocket science. People who practice gratitude tend to have better relationships, improved physical and mental health, greater self-esteem, and remarkable resilience. You can't change anyone's attitude or behavior, but you can work on your own. Before you criticize, condemn, or complain about yourself or someone else, consider the things you can be grateful for. Acknowledge what is good and right in your world, in your person, and in others. Don't waste valuable time hung up on how someone else acts or responds. Focus on you.

Time is the only thing we have in the world that cannot be regenerated. Once it's gone, it's gone. No exchanges, no returns. Time can, however, be hijacked, held for ransom, spent, wasted, and lost in an instant. You are given the apportioned 24 hours in a day, but there are no rollover minutes. You don't get to bargain with time. The only way to save time is to invest it wisely in what sparks joy and peace.

Address unproductive daily habits that rob you of your time. Audit yourself by keeping a log of how you spend your day for 30 days. Review the information to see where you wasted time, how often someone hijacked your time, and where you can invest time more productively. Do you need to carve out more time for the people you love? How long and how often do you scroll through social media or binge-watch streaming programs? An argument with someone about something that really doesn't matter in the larger scheme of things is also a waste of time. At the end of the day, does it really matter which way you put the toilet paper on the roller? You have to pull it off and wipe your backside either way.

Instead of focusing on the trivial, relish small pleasures—how your heart melts when your grandchild smiles at you for the first time, how delicious your mom's homemade spaghetti and fresh garlic bread tastes, the way trees sway in the autumn wind as their leaves swirl to the ground. Life is full of unexpected, wonderful things. Make a habit of focusing on what's in front of your face to get the most out of the time you have.

Habits are the things that make and break us. Very few things happen suddenly. Many of the things we struggle with are the result of habit. Avoidance, procrastination, perfectionism, nail-biting, smoking, and overeating are all habits built over time that keep us stuck in negative patterns of behavior. These patterns imprint on your brain, affecting every area of your life. The way you do one thing is the way you do everything. You put off doing that report the same way you put off clearing that shelf. You avoid speaking up for yourself at a meeting and at the doctor's office. You love browsing through antique shops and keeping old things.

Habits are the brain's way of helping us navigate everyday life. It's great to have them if they're working for you. The ones you have to watch for are the ones working against you. Changing a habit can be difficult. The key is to replace an old habit with a new one. To start, write down two or three bad habits you'd like to replace. Then, identify why you do those things. Do you reach for food when you're sad, stressed, anxious, or bored? Do you go for a walk, browse social media, or play a computer game as a distraction from a problem? Do you treat people badly when you're tired? Our habits are activated by various things going on in our lives and how we feel about them. They operate on a continual loop in our brain. Breaking this chain is challenging but not impossible.

The way to make big changes is not by setting high goals, but by breaking them down into smaller micro habits (Nawaz, 2020). Big goals are harder to achieve than bite-sized ones. To make a big shift, start with small goals. Open three pieces of mail a day and toss, answer, or shred them. Just focus on three a day for a while until it becomes a habit. Then, add two more until that becomes a habit. You don't have to take big steps. Take just a few at a time, like toddlers learning to walk. Fall down six times; get up seven.

The beauty of a micro habit is that it can be achieved with little effort. Global CEO coach, speaker, and writer Sabina Nawaz suggests the following tips to help you succeed in establishing micro habits (Nawaz, 2020).

- **Master the minimums.** What's the easiest possible thing you can do? Aim for the simplest possibility. Want to declutter your closet? Open it and stare at it, and then walk away. Keep doing that until you feel disgusted or get tired of looking at it in the shape it's in. Nawaz explains, you will know you have truly reached the level of a micro habit when you say, "That's so ridiculously small, it's not worth doing." Take it to the next level by setting a date on your calendar to begin decluttering. Look at your closet and that date every day. In doing so, you are training your brain to respond differently. You are slowly and methodically rerouting the circuitry.

- **Piggyback on a daily task.** Combine your new habit with something you already do daily. Meditate while your coffee is brewing. Listen to audiobooks while driving to work. Take a few deep breaths while you're waiting at the checkout line in the supermarket. Piggybacking a new task on an old one limits distractions.
- **Track your progress.** Tracking equals accountability. Set your goal and create a list. Did you do the thing you set out to do today? Check "yes" or "no."
- **Hold steady for a long time.** Don't add anything new to your micro habit until you get a "yes" every day for at least two weeks straight. If you're bored with it by then, increase by no more than 10%. If you've been reading a paragraph a night, read an additional sentence or two. Overdoing it will bring discouragement and possible regression.
- **Seek someone to hold you accountable.** Get together with three or four friends who also want to make changes in their lifestyle and keep each other accountable. It's a win-win situation for everyone involved, and it increases morale and motivation.

Layer small daily habits on top of each other, and you'll soon achieve the goals you have been trying to reach for decades.

POSITIVITY AND THE PERFECT DAY

Remember that perfect day you wrote about in the beginning. What's the distance between where you want to go and where you are now? It's easier to answer this question if you've been gauging your progress. Your initial vision is subject to change. What was perfect for you at first may have changed during the decluttering and organizing process. You may have since decided to redo your entire bathroom. The old sofa with the weathered seats that your grandmother gave you may have since been replaced by an oversized chair or sexy love seat. Is there more room in your garage? Are you more comfortable with surprise guests? Are your significant other and your children more helpful around the house? Is everyone more adept at understanding the concept of everything having a place and everything falling neatly into that space?

Not there yet? No worries. You are closer than you were when you got started. Celebrate how far you've come, even if it's only a little way. Fine tune your road map. Reimagine what you need to tweak to get where you want to be. You now have the tools to do what you may have thought impossible when you first started. Every step you took along the way counts. Celebrate that.

We live in a world of uncertainty. You are not going to be able to control everything. Settle that. You will get sick, tired, or both at the same time. Stuff will happen in your life or the lives of those you love that knocks everything off-kilter. You may have to start all over, but this time you won't be starting from scratch. Go back to your vision every two or three months and tweak as necessary.

Failure is never final. It is a learning experience if we use the knowledge we have gained from it. How are you feeling? Are you less stressed? Are you getting more work done? Do you have fewer headaches? How are you sleeping? Did that manic twitch in your left eye that made people think you were making a pass at them stop being a problem? If so, you are on your way to recovering your authentic self. Your life can now begin again.

CONCLUSION

Is life still chaotic for Laura after implementing all the ideas and suggestions in these chapters? Chaos is par for the course when raising teenagers, but by reducing the clutter, organizing the spaces, creating systems that work, and setting personal boundaries, she is reaping the benefits. Family and work life are far less stressed. She has more time and headspace to do the things she really wants to do. She's picked up her watercolors and is painting again like she did when she was a child.

You've come to the end of the book but not the end of your journey. There will still be loads of laundry. Loud neighbors, coworkers, friends, and relatives may still get on your nerves. But step-by-step, you are reclaiming your sanity, becoming more powerful and productive, and creating much needed space for yourself in a new and ever-changing world. Remember some key rules to stay motivated on your path:

CONCLUSION

- Personal peace triumphs over perfection.
- It's okay to take the long road. This isn't a race.
- Failure is not final. It's just a way station on the journey to your destination. Rome wasn't built in a day. It took sustained action and a couple epic fails.
- Clutter can steal your time, energy, space, money, relationships, and sense of well-being. Don't let it. After all, you wouldn't knowingly let a thief come into your house and rob you blind.
- If you are feeling trapped by it, it owns you, not the other way around.
- Emotional attachment doesn't mean an item is necessary or good for you.
- Though they are useful for organization and storage, too many containers can cause chaos. Stay clear of the container cluster.
- Somebody needs your and your family's stories. Don't be afraid to share your memories and mementos with the world.
- Change is inevitable. Don't resist the paradigm shift. The freedom, new relationships, and emotional and physical healing will be worth it.
- Enjoy the journey.

Minimalism is about so much more than decluttering, buying less, and living a scaled-down lifestyle. Releasing myself from the madness of my cluttered life was about finding myself again. I didn't just release material goods and emotions. I allowed myself to escape from the confinement of the things that were holding me hostage, to live more authentically, and to align myself more with who I am at my core. My personal philosophy is, "It's never too late to have a new beginning in life." Scaling down your life is

CONCLUSION

about learning to love yourself enough to give yourself the space to truly ROCK your midlife season!

You've got this!

Cat x

* **Don't forget your FREE gift to help you begin your decluttering journey!**

The **30 Day Love your Home Decluttering Challenge** will help you take action on the principles you read in this book, with 30 days of email prompts to help you tackle the clutter in your home.

As well, you'll receive a complimentary ebook when you register, along with another surprise along the way. Declutter your entire home in 30 days or collect the prompts and go at your own speed.

It's my gift to help you get started on your decluttering adventure!

Start your own 30 Day Love your Home Decluttering Challenge at this link:
https://iheahavq.pages.infusionsoft.net/

REFERENCES

Ambardekar, N. (2021, March 7). How clutter can affect your health. *WebMD.* https://www.webmd.com/balance/ss/slideshow-clutter-affects-health

Bateman, J., & Rodionova, Z. (2022, March 25). 8 things a decluttering expert never has in their bedroom. *Good Housekeeping.* https://www.goodhousekeeping.com/uk/house-and-home/declutter-your-home/a575013/bedroom-organisation-advice/

Bouchardeau, C., & Delarosa, M. (2008, March 26). The tortured lives of people who can't throw things out. *ABC News.* https://abcnews.go.com/Health/story?id=2790669&page=1

Brauer, V. (2016, February 24). 5 challenges of being a minimalist. *No Sidebar.* https://nosidebar.com/minimalist-challenges/

Brown, B. (2018, October 15). Clear is kind. Unclear is unkind. *Brene' Brown.* https://brenebrown.com/articles/2018/10/15/clear-is-kind-unclear-is-unkind/

Carlson, M. (2016, February 24). 12 extremely easy ways to declutter your bathroom. *Elbow Room.* https://www.clutter.com/blog/posts/declutter-bathroom/

Cherry, K. (2021, July 30). How multitasking affects productivity and brain health. *Verywell Mind.* https://www.verywellmind.com/multitasking-2795003

Cherry, K. (2021, February 20). What is survivor's guilt. *Verywell Mind.* https://www.verywellmind.com/survivors-guilt-4688743

Chrissy. (2022, February 14). Decluttering guilt - 5 brilliant reasons to let it go! *Organise My House.* https://organisemyhouse.com/decluttering-guilt/

REFERENCES

ClutterBug. (2021, October 12). *15 things to declutter from your bathroom - Week two declutter bootcamp* [Video]. YouTube. https://www.youtube.com/watch?v=1lDPHVPsMB0&t=462s

Combiths, S. (2015, September 10). Why does getting rid of stuff feel so good? *Apartment Therapy.* https://www.apartmenttherapy.com/why-does-getting-rid-of-stuff-feel-so-good-223176

Dubin, A. (2022, January 19). 25 laundry room organization hacks to make your life easier. *Woman's Day.* https://www.womansday.com/home/organizing-cleaning/g854/organize-your-laundry-room/?slide=17

Hide-away Storage. (2020, December 23). Decluttering 101: Keep, donate, or throw away? *Hideaway Storage Blog Site.* https://www.hideawaystorage.com/blog/keep-toss-or-donate-a-simple-guide/

Hines, S. (2019, January 16). 10 things a decluttering expert never has in their living room. *Good Housekeeping.* https://www.goodhousekeeping.com/uk/house-and-home/declutter-your-home/a577514/how-to-declutter-living-room/

Larkin, E. (2022a, September 12). 4 smart ways to declutter your bedroom. *The Spruce.* https://www.thespruce.com/cutting-clutter-in-your-bedroom-2647994

Larkin, E. (2022b, September 12). 10 ways to let go of sentimental clutter. *The Spruce.* https://www.thespruce.com/get-rid-of-sentimental-clutter-4126430

Love, J. (2019, August 26). How to organize a drop zone in under 15 minutes. *Rooms Need Love.* https://www.roomsneedlove.com/2019/08/26/organize-a-drop-zone/

Lustbader, W. (2022, March 30). How to throw things away. *Psychology Today.* https://www.psychologytoday.com/intl/blog/life-gets-better/202203/how-throw-things-away

Mayo Clinic Staff. (2018). Hoarding disorder - Symptoms and causes. *Mayo Clinic.* https://www.mayoclinic.org/diseases-conditions/hoarding-disorder/symptoms-causes/syc-20356056

REFERENCES

Modijefsky, G. (2021, September 8). The dangers of information overload and how to prevent it. *Workspace 365*. https://workspace365.net/en/the-dangers-of-information-overload-and-how-to-prevent-it

Mom Can Fix It. (2021, September 14). *Don't make these 11 mistakes with garage organization!* [Video]. YouTube. https://www.youtube.com/watch?v=Qih10gVjdD8

Napier, N. K. (2014, May 12). The myth of multitasking. *Psychology Today*. https://www.psychologytoday.com/us/blog/creativity-without-borders/201405/the-myth-multitasking

Nawaz, S. (2020, January 20). To achieve big goals, start with small habits. *Harvard Business Review*. https://hbr.org/2020/01/to-achieve-big-goals-start-with-small-habits

Perrine, J. (2020, January 22). 5 types of office clutter that kill your productivity. *All Things Admin*. https://www.allthingsadmin.com/5-types-office-clutter/

Rao Ph.D, P. M. S. (2020, October 12). The power of visualization: convert your vision into reality. *CEOWORLD Magazine*. https://ceoworld.biz/2020/10/12/the-power-of-visualization-convert-your-vision-into-reality/

Reagan, A. (2015, February 10). A brief history of the bedroom. *Porch*. https://porch.com/advice/history-bedroom

Sander, L. (2019, January 22). Marie Kondo tidying up: This is what clutter does to your brain and body. *Newsweek*. https://www.newsweek.com/tidying-marie-kondo-clutter-netflix-life-changing-magic-tidying-mental-health-1299938

Simple Lionheart Life. (2021, September 29). The negative effects of clutter: 12 ways your stuff is stealing from you! *Simple Lionheart Life*. https://simplelionheartlife.com/negative-effects-of-clutter/

Stillman, J. (2021, April 19). The 5 types of clutter that are destroying your peace of mind. *Inc.com*. https://www.inc.com/jessica-stillman/the-5-types-of-clutter-that-are-destroying-your-peace-of-mind.html

REFERENCES

TEDx Talks. (2017, April 19). From clutter to clarity | Kerry Thomas | TEDx-Ashburn [Video]. YouTube. https://www.youtube.com/watch?v=Crsdo IOGCRw&t=703s

Thomas, C. (2009, June 4). Monday morning heart attacks – and other weird facts about women's heart disease. *Heart Sisters*. https://myheartsisters.org/2009/06/04/monday-morning-heart-attacks/

Van Pelt, K. (2022, August). How to organize a living room. *The Spruce*. https://www.thespruce.com/how-to-organize-a-living-room-6386097

Watson, K. (2018, September 27). What is sensory overload? Healthline; *Healthline Media*. https://www.healthline.com/health/sensory-overload

ABOUT CAT

Cat Coluccio is an Author, a Reinvention Coach, the host of the **Rocking Midlife®** Podcast and Community - *and a champion of midlife women.*

A qualified Educator, Personal Trainer and Life Coach, Cat is passionate about seeing women empowered to stop procrastinating, clear their internal and external clutter so that they can identify their values and goals, take intentional action and build purposeful lives and businesses.

At home speaking on both live or virtual stages, Cat has been a featured guest on numerous international podcasts and summits, as well as in national print publications, television and radio shows.

A transplanted Australian, she resides in New Zealand with her husband, children and grandson, along with far too many cats, chooks and sheep. She's partial to a glass of prosecco and a laugh with friends, good chocolate, great books, and lives by her personal philosophy: *"It's never too late to have a new beginning in life."* To learn more, please visit: www.catcoluccio.com

Check out Cat's other books!

Your Midlife Side Hustle!

The blueprint to help take you from an idea, to creating, to launching, to scaling your own passion-fuelled, purposeful and profitable online business!

Available on Amazon

21 Hacks to ROCK your Midlife – *release the past, dare to dream and create your legacy!*

Cat's 7 stage model takes you through the process of releasing the past and accepting who you are now, so that you can determine the purposeful life and legacy you want to create going forward!

Available on Amazon

21 Hacks to Rock Your Life - stop procrastinating, do that thing, and live your life on purpose!

An entertaining and engaging guide to taking control of your life so you can *stop procrastinating, get unstuck, and live your best life 'On Purpose' today!*

Available on Amazon

21 Hacks to Rock your Life Teen Edition - stop stuffing around, get focused and create a life that rocks!

Give the teen in your life a step up with this handy book that will help them learn how to focus on the things that *really* matter and take action to create their rocking life!

Available on Amazon

Connect with Cat Coluccio on Social Media

https://www.facebook.com/CatColuccio/
https://instagram.com/catcoluccio
https://www.youtube.com/c/CatColuccio

Printed in Great Britain
by Amazon